ASHLEY ADAMS

the Other Side of the Door

Behind the **lies** and the **secrets** we keep

This book is a memoir. It reflects the author's recollections over time. Certain names and identifying characteristics have been changed to protect privacy, whether or not so noted in the text. Conversations in the book are written from the author's memory and journal entries.

Cover design: Anointing Productions
Editor: Mair Downing
Author headshot: Shine Photography by Elle Lappan

Paperback ISBN-13: 978-1-7344087-0-6

To my children, who have helped me find immeasurable strength.

Table of Contents

Introduction   1

Chapter 1: Where it all began   5

Chapter 2: And baby makes three   15

Chapter 3: It all falls apart   23

Chapter 4: The web of lies unravels   33

Chapter 5: Letting someone else take over   49

Chapter 6: Happy birthday, Ryan   57

Chapter 7: Settling into a new routine   71

Chapter 8: Protecting the assets   81

Chapter 9: Navigating   91

Chapter 10: Learning to heal   97

Chapter 11: Disappointment and letdown   103

Chapter 12: Single moments   115

Chapter 13: You're dead to me   119

Chapter 14: What's a family?   125

Chapter 15: Letting God lead   133

Chapter 16: How does the Bachelorette do it?   149

Chapter 17: Me again   161

Chapter 18: Everything changes   169

Chapter 19: Moving forward   189

Chapter 20: Meeting him   199

Chapter 21: Falling in love again   211

Chapter 22: Risking it all   217

Chapter 23: Crazy girl   225

Chapter 24: Forever and ever   235

Chapter 25: Party of 5   249

Introduction

If you write, you get to turn your lessons into your legacy.
-Taylor Swift, Time100 Gala
April 23, 2019

It's funny how you can look back on a past event in your life and realize its impact years later. And it hit me randomly one day just before Thanksgiving thirteen years later while I was walking down the hall at work. Since I knew the draft of this book was looming, I had to pull out my phone and write it down so I wouldn't forget it—because as I get older and busier, I forget the important stuff ALL THE TIME! (I hope it's not just me.)

When I was in college, I did my last semester abroad on a ship that sailed us around the world while we took classes in between visiting other countries. But two weeks into our trip, we had what is affectionately known to our shipboard community as Wave Day, where we were left (temporarily) stranded in the middle of the Pacific Ocean. This near-death experience left me both fearless for my future (I never get nervous on a plane because I figure you probably only have one major brush with disaster, and mine has already happened) but also totally afraid of being alone. I always thought my life was supposed to follow "the plan" and I needed to get a job, get married, and have kids. Wave Day created a fear in me that made me need to achieve all of those goals NOW. And, I was so afraid I'd end up alone if I didn't end up with Jeff, my boyfriend at the time.

I started that trip in love with a man I never saw a future with, just a college boyfriend that I'd say goodbye to when the time came. And then, my brain did a complete one-eighty after Wave Day. I found a way to focus on all the good in this man, even though there were plenty of red flags that should have told a very smart twenty-two-year-old to slow down and take a more objective look at the situation. *Was this really the man for me?*

And at the end of the day, I decided that two things mattered to me above all else—he made me laugh, and I knew he'd be a great dad one day. The rest, we'd work our way through.

Unfortunately, things didn't turn out that way, and a happy ending wasn't in the cards for us. With two little kids at home, ages one and three, I was all alone and couldn't find any books on the market for how to be a single mom to toddlers or how to explain to someone so small that dad wasn't coming home.

I was incredibly judgmental about divorce prior to going through my own experience, and even now, I find some judgement creeping in—even though I've led a divorce support group twice and know that (almost) every story is really painful and justified. The simple reminder to be kind to others floats through my mind. You never know what someone else is going through.

This is my story. What started out as something for single moms evolved to a memoir of the crazy things I've been though, the lessons learned along the way, and how I got to the place I am today—which is, spoiler alert, spending the summer on my couch snuggling through my maternity leave with a new baby.

Life isn't perfect, but that tiny human is. And I'm so grateful for every experience I had over the last ten years.

I learned that there's no such thing as a happy ending. But it's important to remain optimistic and hold on to hope when things look bleak and scary. That, somehow down the line, you're going to come out of this blackhole, and life is going to feel good again.

One day, you'll wake up and realize you haven't cried for a whole week. Then, a whole month. You'll realize that you have the energy to devote to more than just your emotions. That you can be a good parent, a good friend, and a good daughter again. And life will *feel* good. It won't be perfect, and there's no promise that heartbreak won't come again. But when the moment is good, live in it.

For me, music has always been a huge part of my life. Concerts, song lyrics, melodies. I love how they transport me, sympathize with me, and somehow vocalize exactly how I feel. I can hear certain songs and immediately be taken back to a moment in time, good or bad. You'll see that referenced throughout the story.

I like to think I'm healed from the trauma of my first marriage, but then a song will come on when I'm alone in my car, and I find myself in tears. It feels like a way to keep healing and learning from my past. It reminds me how strong I am and what an incredibly blessed life I've been given.

I decided to publish this book now because when my brother-in-law told me I should write a book about my experiences, there wasn't a single book I could find that told me how to deal with divorce when the kids are less than six or so. It was like divorce with kids that age didn't exist. It made me feel even worse—like, do people not get divorced this early? Am I such a failure that self-help books aren't even available? Should I have been able to stick it out until they were at least both out of diapers?

I hope that if you can see yourself within these pages that it helps you realize you aren't alone. So many go through what I went through, and while our situations may not be the same, the story, the feeling, the pain—I find that we all generally go through the same stuff. And it helps to know you aren't alone.

Chapter 1

Where it all began

I had a brief stint as a waitress during my third year of college. I liked getting the steady paycheck, but I was a terrible waitress. I didn't drink wine yet and couldn't open a bottle in front of customers to save my life, and even though I could sweet talk with the guests and ask how their golf game was or if they'd been at the last football game in the rain, it was a country club, so there was no tipping. Therefore, I tried to get as many lunch shifts as I could. Fewer guests and less booze to stress me out.

It was on one of my first shifts that I met Jeff, who'd gone to culinary school several years earlier and had been working at the country club for a while. He kept me fed in the early days— pasta, omelets, maybe even steak on a good night. And he taught me how to love cooked spinach (the secret is lots of mozzarella cheese).

After he asked me out for the first time, he stood me up. I paced the creaky floors of my apartment for a solid hour before finally accepting he wasn't coming. That should have been my indicator of things to come, but I gave him the benefit of the doubt for whatever stupid excuse he had used. And then, he did it *again*. There was a lot of groveling that time, and it was a while before I was willing to give him a *third* try—and it was something really low key that involved other people, so it was no big deal if he bailed yet again.

So, I know that, all of these failed first dates should mean that we never even started dating. But he had these piercing blue eyes and wore this khaki visor at work where his eyes peered through in a way that just made me melt. And he was older, so obviously he had his life together, right?

We were together a little over a year when I left for my semester abroad. I was in love for sure, but I also wasn't thinking he was my forever either. Even so, with my need to wrap my life up in a tidy little bow, we started talking long term and moving in together after I got back. But being a rule follower, I didn't want to live together until we were engaged. I was basically setting us up to rush into marriage.

We got engaged in November, right before Thanksgiving. The holidays were exciting, and it was fun to be the first of my friends to show off a fiancé and plan a wedding. My mom and I went in to full planning mode, looking at color schemes (pink and black) and thinking about where to go to try on dresses.

During our engagement, Jeff's cousin died in a car crash. A cousin he idolized and who had very recently started AA. Jeff and I had been unaware of his struggle with alcohol, so Jeff thought it was crazy to think his cousin had a problem and refused to buy into it.

Instead, Jeff started drinking a lot as his coping mechanism to get through the grief. I was really concerned about him and hated who he was when he drank too much. But he was in so much pain from losing his cousin, and I knew drinking was a pretty common way to cope in the face of loss. So, I circled back to that over and over during our engagement to rationalize what was going on with him.

It never struck me at the time that Jeff could actually be an *alcoholic*. Plus, we met when I was twenty and was drinking like most college kids. I don't know that I would have been able to recognize signs of alcoholism in someone.

Still, I was nervous about getting married. Did he really have the drive to open up a restaurant like he said? Were the video games really going to disappear down the road when kids came along? Could he manage his money?

Being the optimist I am, I just chalked it all up to nerves and not that something was actually wrong. When I questioned if I should go through with it, I knew I didn't have the guts to back out. I'd gone too far down the path to admit anything was a mistake. Plus, what if it wasn't? What if this was just a hardship Jeff was facing, and he was going to turn out just fine? I wanted my happy ending to start. We were buying a house together. Our lives were already getting tied together, and I didn't know how to stop the train—or if I wanted to.

Our wedding was so beautiful. It was a chilly day in October, but there wasn't a cloud in the sky. Friends and family filled the lush, green lawn of a gorgeous old estate out in the country. It had white columns on the house and a stone fountain as our backdrop, with leaves the perfect shades or orange and red in the Blue Ridge mountains.

The afternoon ceremony was officiated by a very sweet, non-denominational woman who let us choose our readings, our rituals, and music throughout. We had some of my best friends as bridesmaids, and his brother and cousins were groomsmen. You see, even though Jeff was undeniably personable and likable, he didn't actually have any real friends. He wasn't social and never developed relationships throughout school or work that led to deep connections. He was so fun around my friends that I remember thinking we just needed to start making 'couple friends' once we were married, and he'd start to find other men to hang out with.

Jeff did make one friend a while after we moved, and he started a new job. He was a young guy named Patrick, working part-time while he went to college in town. Patrick ended up being a great friend to him, all the way to the end. He was a kind soul and had enough in common with Jeff that they could hang out and have a good time—usually at home with beer. He tried to talk sense into Jeff as he started going downhill. Like me, he struggled to know what was enabling and what was supportive.

Looking back, I don't remember having a lot of problems in our marriage until I got pregnant with our first child. But that wasn't true. When you're the first of your friends to get married, there aren't a lot of people you can go to when you have a problem. I made the choice to settle down at 23, and then when life got hard just a couple years later, my life felt like it was falling apart. And I wasn't brave enough to talk to anyone about what was going on—not without risking huge embarrassment or feeling like an absolute failure.

One of the things I did back then was journal—whenever Jeff and I had a big fight or there was something that was tearing my heart apart. At least by getting it out of my head and on to paper, I had some release. And at the time, it was enough.

My first entry was written just two years in to my marriage, during one of our low points. I remember those days—when he would drink a handle of bourbon in a five-day work week, leaving brown paper bags stashed all over the house from the mini bottles he bought. Back when he constantly yelled at me and told me how selfish I was. For nearly six years, he was able to function as an alcoholic.

I don't think it's a good sign to start writing a journal when all you have to say is negative, but since that's where I am in life with no one I can talk to, this is where it begins. Marriage is not what I expected or hoped for. I am sad more than I am happy. I feel underappreciated. I feel lonely because I don't know anyone who can relate. And I just plain don't know where to turn.

Jeff is an alcoholic. I know he is, and I know he has had a problem since before we got married. I am embarrassed for him and I am embarrassed for me. I know that's why I've never confessed our problems to anyone because they all stem from his drinking. He thinks I am controlling and that I belittle him. Mostly, I do those things because he drinks. He is irresponsible and has no responsibilities outside of going to work. And even that, he can't be bothered to be sure he gets his 40 hours because there is always at least a few hours of vacation that gets put in there to add up to 40. It's ridiculous. I completely understand that he is jealous of my work schedule and the money I bring in, but I don't know how to get him to think of us as equal partners, and if he feels inferior, why he can't do something extra to make himself feel more important.

Let me pause here to give some additional clarity. First, reading this back more than ten years later, I truly can't believe that I knew back then that he was an alcoholic and that things were this bad. Second, I worked in sales at the time and had a company car and a ton of flexibility with my hours. Jeff took this to mean that my job was slack and generally treated me like I wasn't a valuable employee because of that. In my first year of work, I was the #1 salesperson on my team—*nationally.* When I went to a new company a year after that, I was in the top third. And I was starting to bring home good money—significantly more than him.

I know that I am controlling. I know that I am hard on him. I try to keep my mouth shut and let him do his thing, but then I get so fed up that I blow up and we fight. He comes home, changes right into comfy clothes and sits on the couch playing video games until dinner. Maybe once a week we will eat dinner together, but then it's right back to our separate rooms (We had two living rooms, so I generally watched tv in one, and him in the other — something I deeply regret looking back, and I tell all my friends, **watch tv together**).

Anytime we try to make the effort to be together more, things are really good. I enjoy being with him and watching movies or sports or eating dinner, but our intentions never make it past a week—both ready to go back to doing what we want to do.

And I am so selfish. I want a baby so bad, and even though I hate my husband more than I love him these days, I refuse to believe that at 25 years old I should even have the thoughts of divorce. I believe in marriage through the good and the bad, and even though a baby never fixes things, I know it would make Jeff grow up and be more mature and responsible. But the more we fight, the less I want a baby with him. I feel like there is a reason I have not gotten pregnant yet. What if Jeff is not the person I spend my life with? So often I really do want to start over. I want to go back to the way I felt when we first lived together and I knew that something was off and the fighting was not fun. But I thought that it came with the territory. I didn't know if the fights were normal. I didn't know if they were just fears about the wedding. I should have listened. I don't think I should have ever married him. But I do love him. I love that he makes me laugh every day. We are so passionate in our love and hate for each other, and I don't know which is stronger. These days it is definitely the hate.

The drinking is the cause of our problems almost 100% of the time. But he doesn't see his drinking as a problem. He sees me as the problem for being too controlling and not appreciating that he is trying to cut back. I'm sorry, but he's not cutting back at all. He may definitely be "trying" but the same amount of alcohol is consumed every week—a handle of bourbon is gone in 5 days or less—Plus all the beer he has when we go to my parents', a football game, or that he simply buys at the store to enjoy. Tonight I suggested he switch to beer exclusively because at least if he just drinks beer, he's not as mean or pouty.

Tonight our fight started because he got mad at me for assuming he was going to bed when he'd turned off the tv/lights in his room, had poured a glass of water, gone upstairs, taken off his clothes and came back down in his boxers. Then I told him he was drunk. That was the bomb to set him off. He is so selfish when it comes to my feelings on this issue, and I really can't understand why. I know I need to seek professional help on this problem, but I'm so afraid to face it for real. When it's just me and him, no one else needs to know that he's a mess or that we are in a bad place in life so young.

The first time I really confronted him about it, he blamed it on his cousin's death. I understood that at the time, but it's been over two years since his death, and Jeff still refuses to believe that his cousin was in AA or had a drinking problem. I would think that in a strange way, Jeff would like the connection to him—that they both have this problem. But I think he likes having a different connection—Jeff wants it to be the one he remembers of him—the drinking part. The fun part. The fun times they had together just before he died.

You guys, even though that was written two years into my marriage when I don't even remember having marital problems, I could have written it at year eight too, and almost all of it would have still applied. He never grew out of any of the issues that were causing me stress and anxiety, and it took one moment of temporary insanity that led me to finally face it all and leave him.

It's amazing the lengths our minds will go to in order to protect us. Truly, in reading back on some of my journal entries—entries I wrote during only our most intense and traumatic fights—I don't even remember them. I can picture it all because it's the same life I led off and on for eight years, but if someone asked me about Jeff or my marriage, I would have believed myself if I told you it was mostly good up until the end, when it came crashing down.

Chapter 2

And baby makes three

There I remember things starting to go south was in the summer of 2009—after I suffered a miscarriage. We'd been trying for a few months, and when I got that double line, I was filled with all the excitement in the world. Again, none of my friends had babies yet, and I hadn't become jaded with the harsh facts about getting pregnant and *staying* pregnant. I didn't know it could take months and months of purposely trying for a baby to make it happen, and I didn't know how common it was for that positive test to end in a miscarriage.

In the ultrasound room for the first time, Jeff and I stared at that little blob on the screen, mesmerized. I reminded the tech to take some photos for me.

"Are you sure about the date of your last period?" she asked. "The baby is only measuring five and half weeks. There's no heartbeat yet."

I didn't give that conversation a second thought—we were just a bit early for the appointment, I guess. After the "fun" part of our appointment was done and we'd seen the baby on the screen, I sent Jeff on his way so he could get to work, and I said I'd be fine waiting for the doctor on my own since the rest was going to be pretty standard stuff.

It wasn't standard stuff though. In all of our excitement and naivety, I didn't connect the dots that something was wrong. I was devastated. There was no heartbeat because there'd been no fetal growth. The baby should have been measuring closer to seven or eight weeks, and the doctor told me that if I didn't miscarry on my own in the next few days, I would need to schedule surgery to remove everything.

I left like I'd been hit by a truck. I was so shocked and didn't know what to do. I called Jeff and told him, and he met me back at home. I called my mom and she left work and came over. I felt so numb.

And the thing about a miscarriage is that it happens so early that usually there's no outward support from work or friends because it's not news that's typically shared.

"Wait until twelve weeks" has to be the stupidest advice ever. If those early weeks are the riskiest, then doesn't it make more sense to share with your day-to-day network in case you do need their support and sympathy?

I was supposed to go to Charleston, SC, with a bunch of girlfriends for Memorial Day weekend, but my surgery was scheduled the following week and I was advised to "stay close to home" in case I started bleeding. We spent most of the weekend on the couch, wallowing. One evening though, Jeff and I tagged along with my parents to an outdoor event downtown where this new band was playing who had recently hit it big with their song *Chicken Fried*.

I've seen Zac Brown Band quite a few times over the years, and I still get a bit emotional when that song plays, particularly the last line of the chorus:

> *See the love in my woman's eyes*
> *Feel the touch of a precious child*
> *And know a mother's love.*

At the time, the song was about longing—for this child I was losing, the mother I wasn't about to become.

But today, the song not only brings me back to that moment, it reminds me how much I love and adore my kids and would do anything for them.

A few weeks later, we had a trip to Las Vegas planned with Jeff's brother and wife. I love Vegas, and I was really looking forward to the carefree weekend and drinking away a bit of the pain. But on day one of that trip, my sister-in-law Beth told us that she was pregnant. About six or seven weeks, if I remember correctly. You see, Beth is a recovering alcoholic, so at that early stage, she really didn't need to tell us. I wouldn't have suspected a thing since she wouldn't have been drinking on the trip anyway. They knew about my miscarriage, and I felt so angry that they didn't wait until after the trip to share their good news with us. We were still so raw in our pain.

Of course, I *was* really happy for them, but my pain from not being able to get pregnant easily was raw and always present, so it stung. By Thanksgiving, we still weren't pregnant, and they were going to be visiting us. I knew I wasn't going to be able to deal with seeing her growing bump or be able to smile as she told me about all their preparations.

I cried all the time, so I went to my primary care doctor and asked about an anti-depressant—something I'd always been taught growing up that I should avoid.

Thankfully, the stigma of mental health is lessening now, and I'm so glad I took the plunge to try out Prozac for a few months. It was a really weird sensation for me—I'd be in a situation that I knew should be making me sad or making me cry, but it didn't. I could feel my brain blocking the pain for me, and it was so fascinating—and so scary—to get a glimpse at its power.

I was only on the medicine for two months before I got pregnant again. I did all the early blood-work to make sure my levels were rising properly. When we went for our first ultrasound, I was a bundle of nerves.

I told the tech, "The last time we were here, we had a miscarriage, so we're pretty anxious."

As soon as we started the exam, she said, "You can relax. I see a heartbeat."

We both let out a huge sigh of relief and a handful of tears. She also printed about thirty pictures for us to take, so I quickly learned that's the difference between a bad ultrasound and a good one. If your tech isn't taking pictures for you, you're in trouble.

I was a nervous wreck my first trimester. I didn't work out at all because I was convinced I'd contributed to the miscarriage by doing heavy cardio the first time. I mostly sat around and gained twelve pounds in those first few weeks—on my way to sixty! So, I wasn't feeling great about myself, and Jeff's drinking was picking back up.

I was in the middle of getting my masters too, and taking classes four nights a week while still working full-time during the day. It was a grueling schedule, but at my current pace, I'd be on my last two classes when the baby arrived.

This could have all been manageable with Jeff's support, but he spent his evenings getting drunk in front of the tv and was usually asleep by the time I got home each night.

Sometimes, I could tell he'd been drinking, but only if he was sloppy—leaving half full cups with bourbon on the table or leaving liquor-sized paper bags lying around. Usually, he played it off as just being tired, and at first, I believed him. He was an amazing liar. The nights I 'caught' him were the nights that he explained away as one-offs.

On top of being incredibly busy with school, I interviewed for a new job at twenty weeks pregnant. Since it was my first baby, I wasn't showing much and easily hid my bump. I didn't tell them about being pregnant until they offered me the job.

The new job was a risk—a small startup at the time, in the early stages of the daily deal craze. The benefits and flexibility were great though, and I would be working from home a lot. This was great for the pregnant woman who didn't want to venture into the heat more than necessary. But for Jeff, it added to his annoyance with my so-called life of luxury.

He also had a hard time seeing my body change, and a pregnant body wasn't for him. Although he never said a thing to me, his lack of affection and attention left me really hating being pregnant and the way I looked. And without a physical connection, he drifted further away.

Sometime in my first or second trimester, I criticized something about drinking that he took as a personal attack. Then, he got pissed. I don't know if he had intentions of hitting me or scaring me or something else, but I ran up the stairs and locked myself in our guest room while he yelled through the door, banging on it until he got tired. I wrote it off as a one-off incident and tried not to let it get to me or harp on him for it the next day. It was basically forgotten.

When I was almost nine months pregnant, I woke him one evening from a stupor and told him to go up to bed and get out of my hair. He stumbled up the stairs for bed, and he literally

PUNCHED A HOLE IN THE WALL. That's it. Punched the wall and went to bed.

I told my parents that he tripped carrying something up the stairs or some stupid lie that made no sense.

After that night, Jeff said he wanted us to start going out and doing date nights to bring us closer together. I was so happy to hear that he wanted to try and make things better. I begged him to do these things for so long. Somehow, they never came to fruition. We never made the time.

The baby, my amazing daughter Peyton, came a few weeks later and life got even more challenging.

When Peyton was two weeks old, Jeff got really mad at me one night and lost his cool. She was screaming in my arms, but Jeff wouldn't let up, and he shoved me. I locked the door to the bedroom and he still came in. I didn't know what to do so I called his brother—who lived six-hundred miles away. Why? Why was that all my brain could think to do in that moment? Jeff was in a drunken, blind rage. He was frustrated with me for something I don't even remember, and he was making no sense as he yelled at me while I held Peyton tight to my chest.

Chris, his brother, managed to get Jeff on the phone and basically told him to calm the eff down and take a breather.

It did not even dawn on me to call the cops that night! Didn't cross my mind. How messed up is that? It was one of the worst nights of my life, and yet with the exception of Chris, it was something no one ever knew even happened until now.

His temper got so much worse over the years, but that was the only time he ever touched me.

Chapter 3

It all falls apart

Jeff always said we lived in "Ashley's World" and that I controlled everything. He was right; I did. I understood why he felt that way and why it triggered so much anger. He continually let me down any time I gave him any wiggle room, and I never felt like I could relax. I had to be in control.

A big part of his stress and anger at the time came from his lack of confidence with our daughter. When Peyton was a month old, he shooed me away one night so he could take care of her when she started crying. He brought her upstairs and put on music, sang to her, shushed her—and she was still crying. If you've ever been around a baby, you know they cry. And sometimes, all that's going to console them is some milk.

He brought her back downstairs and came in yelling at me, "Why are you just letting me suffer up there? Do you think it's funny?"

It was bizarre. I assumed he would have called me if he wanted me or if he thought she needed to nurse. Instead, he broke down in heavy tears and left the room.

I changed her diaper then asked if he would talk to me. He accused me again of wanting him to sit there and suffer.

"You should have come in! I've never been around a baby, and I don't know what I'm doing."

BINGO.

Here is why he'd been avoiding spending more time with her. He was scared shitless. That whole first month, I thought he just wasn't interested in her.

The next night, Jeff came home from work and offered to take the baby to give me a break. He gave me a big hug, and whispered, "Everything will be okay. Go relax, and I'll watch the baby."

I went upstairs to get some schoolwork done (*remember, I'm still working on that master's!*).

We'd discussed giving the baby a bath around seven. At 7:20, I went downstairs, impressed it was still quiet, and I found him and Peyton asleep. This wouldn't be a problem except he wasn't holding her. She was lying on the couch with nothing to restrain her. Rookie mistake, right? I wasn't mad, but it was stupid.

I didn't get mad until I picked up a Solo cup off the floor, and it still had liquid drops around the cup letting me know it was from tonight—and it reeked of bourbon. Seriously? He just promised me two hours earlier that it wouldn't happen again. HOW could I let this continue? Now, he's put Peyton in harm's way. I tried repeatedly to wake him—shoved the cup in his face, shoved him. No movement. I picked the baby up and hoped he'd notice that. Nothing. I went and bathed her myself, put her to bed, went back downstairs and he was still passed out. All the noise in the world wouldn't wake him—and no matter how tired he was, you could wake him with movement and noise… unless he'd been drinking.

That was the eve of our 4th anniversary, and it was the first time I was willing to wake up and make a change.

We started counseling the next week.

Counseling was tough. We found a younger woman who was no bullshit, and Jeff seemed to like her. We did some sessions together, and he went on his own too. I cried a lot in those sessions trying to get through to Jeff so he would understand how much his drinking impacted me, our relationship, and our family. You could tell he gave it a lot of lip service and didn't feel any guilt or remorse for the pain he was causing me—he was simply defensive.

We talked about his behavior in various situations—ball games where he mostly drank beer versus at home or at weddings where he typically loaded up on hard liquor. It was the first time we rationalized "good" drinking versus "bad" drinking. Beer was okay. Bourbon was bad. Beer was a happy drunk. Bourbon was an angry drunk.

Looking back, I really regret categorizing his drinking in that way. It allowed for excuses—reasons to keep drinking. We set rules around how much bourbon was an acceptable amount. Buying more than one handle a week = bad. Waiting until pay-day for the next one = acceptable. Trying to set rules around drinking is a recipe for disaster for someone who is an alcoholic. At the time, of course, I still hadn't admitted that's what he was. He was just the guy who embarrassed me at parties.

Jeff started individual counseling with our therapist, where I naively thought he'd open up to her more and she'd use her magical therapist skills to get him to realize he had a drinking problem, and he probably needed to stop.

But that was a fantasy. After a couple of months, she told us that she was moving locations and couldn't see us anymore—said we'd be okay.

Thinking about that now, I'm convinced it was because she got a different story from Jeff in his solo sessions that would make our sessions as a couple a waste. Maybe she didn't know how to help us if he wasn't ready or willing to help himself. Because of confidentiality, she couldn't come out and say, "Look, you guys need to talk because Jeff isn't giving the full story."

I guess I appreciate her saving what little money we had, but what I would have appreciated more was a direct approach so I could have been more in tune with the reality of our situation.

Things were pretty rough for us for most of Peyton's first year. The baby thing was hard for Jeff. I could see how much he loved Peyton and loved to play with her, but it was a huge leap in responsibility for him, and he just couldn't do it. As she became less breakable, he became more engaged though. And life as I can remember it got better. The drinking eased up, and he switched to beer more.

That eternal optimist in me assumed the worst was behind us. So naturally, we decided it was time for a bigger house—the "forever house." My new job was going well, and I was bringing in more money. The market had bottomed out, and while we were going to lose money on our home, we were going to get a really good deal on a bigger home. We lucked out with a beautiful five-bedroom home in a neighborhood only a few miles from our current house. And it was at the bottom of our budget— something I was beyond grateful for when Jeff moved out and I could afford to stay put.

When we moved in, life was so good. Jeff was motivated to make our house look good, and it was a newer home, so the maintenance wasn't too stressful. We became great friends with our neighbors who had a son close in age to Peyton, and during the warm nights after the kids were in bed, we'd bring chairs out into the driveway to hang out with wine and beer and the baby monitors. It was the picture-perfect suburban life.

Jeff and I decided (maybe I decided?) we should try and fill up some of those empty rooms. Thankfully, getting pregnant with Ryan was much easier. It was still a long seven months of trying, but my pregnancy was pretty easy since I wasn't going through the heat of summer, and I already set my expectations pretty low for Jeff's support during the whole thing.

Jeff had a great boss, and they'd worked together for years. When his boss left one job, he brought Jeff along to their current place. But suddenly, Jeff was complaining about him a lot. His boss was "always on him" and Jeff often came home frustrated and complaining. Then, they were bought out by another company, and it was downhill from there. Jeff said people were getting fired "for the stupidest things" and he was sure he wouldn't make it for long. He'd started getting written up for things that he thought were unnecessary.

Finally, he came home one day in the spring and let me know he'd been fired. The reason he gave me was that he counted out the cash box without another person present, but I always wonder if it was really that he was counting out money and taking some for himself as a way to be able to buy more booze without me knowing.

I found out long after Jeff had moved out that when he'd been at work, he was always going out to his car and drinking on breaks. It was humiliating to know all of this was happening and I had no idea.

Without a job, and with a new baby coming soon, I set to work to update Jeff's LinkedIn profile and resume, and we ended up finding him a great job with a national food service company. His salary was slightly more than he'd been making at his last job too. Only we had one problem—Jeff hated this new boss.

"She's a dictator."

"She's always on me. She wants me to fail."

The list went on.

When we had our son Ryan in June, she sent us a card and called to congratulate him. She didn't sound evil to me.

And yet, the complaints kept up. Jeff's anxiety was high, and he was having a really hard time staying committed to the job. I told him he couldn't quit unless he found another one. Obviously.

While I was still in the hospital with Ryan, Jeff was totally disengaged and really short-tempered. My mom couldn't take it and confronted him about it after he'd gone home one night. She let him know she didn't like his behavior and the way he was treating me.

I had to hear all about that the next day from Jeff.

"Your mom needs to mind her own business. She doesn't know what she's talking about. Did you put her up to that?"

He was mad at me and assumed I asked her to say something. Of course, nothing could be further from the truth. I didn't want to talk about any of this to anyone at all. Especially, not my poor mom.

I asked her to lay off and not say anything to him again so I wouldn't have to hear about it. That I had it under control.

On our first night home, Jeff must have been drunk. He brought Ryan into our room and instead of laying him on the bed to change him or change him first in the nursery, he put him on my dresser—which was covered in stuff. Three days post-surgery, I had to jump out of bed to take Ryan from him. I don't think I had him help with anymore night shifts after that. Jeff continued to check out.

I knew it was possible to get short term disability by claiming stress and anxiety, so I suggested that Jeff go to his doctor and ask about it.

That was in October, and his doctor wrote him out that day. And even though Jeff had been with this new company for less than six months, he was eligible for disability benefits, and he got *full pay* for twenty-six weeks. For half a year, Jeff stayed home alone or with our baby all day, every day. For six whole months, he sat in front of the tv all day long. And also, apparently, drank.

While on leave, Jeff started doing individual counseling, with a new therapist, and he'd invite me to sessions every now and then. He really wanted things to be better.

One day, I went on my own to talk with his counselor for more guidance on how to handle things. Jeff was currently in a "beer only" drinking phase and I never saw him drink very much, but his behavior made me feel like he was. She wasn't allowed to confirm anything I said or asked, but she offered advice and very clearly said, "I'd listen to your gut on this, and if you think something is happening, it probably is."

One night in late March, I was on the phone with Chris and Beth, my brother and sister-in-law, discussing Jeff's behavior.

"His 'anxiety' is through the roof," I told Beth. "He's on medication for it, and it's making him really shaky all the time, and he throws up every morning."

My sister-in-law, the recovering alcoholic, let me know that when she was drinking heavily at the end, she was throwing up every morning too.

She didn't outright accuse Jeff of heavy drinking, but she suggested, "I'd think about what is happening around you and don't take it at face value."

I didn't have to think about things for long or analyze what my gut was saying.

The next morning while getting ready for work, I walked in on Jeff, in a stained white t-shirt and his athletic shorts, pouring bourbon into a soda can at 7:45AM and I knew our lives were never going to be the same.

Chapter 4

The web of lies unravels

"Oh my God, it's true."

That was all I could muster when my deepest fear slapped me in the face. I couldn't believe he was drinking to start his day. I couldn't believe that it had become so commonplace that I couldn't even tell he was drunk. My mind was racing thinking about the last few months.

He'd been self-destructing for months while on leave from work. Probably longer, but things escalated once that time at home started. I don't want to discount his anxiety, but it was really his alcohol use causing his symptoms. I was completely fooled.

It truly disgusts me to think that for months he drove the kids to and from daycare while drinking. He kept them twice a week to help us save money on childcare. I went away twice for long weekends and left them in his care. His lying and manipulation was amazing. Oscar worthy! He had been so useless around the house, and I truly thought it was his anxiety medication making him vomit every morning and not be able to eat until 2PM. It was his medicine making him sleep the day away. Lose weight. And I was wrong.

It baffles me how I could be so stupid and clueless.

In that moment of discovery, Jeff apologized, and he cried. He told me he wanted to stop if I would help him.

"Please," he begged.

This began his first three days of going through withdrawal. I was too ashamed to tell my mom. I felt like such a failure and thought I'd hear her lecture me with a whole lot of 'I told you so' that I just couldn't stomach.

I stayed in contact with Beth, who was also a doctor, a lot those first two days, relaying symptoms and checking that a trip to the ER wasn't necessary. It was all terrible. He spent his days sweating and shaking and bundled up on the couch. It was like the worst flu symptoms I'd ever seen. Except he'd brought this on himself by poisoning his body. When he moved from the couch, it was just to go to the bathroom and vomit.

I couldn't believe he'd done this to himself, and he was determined that was it. He never wanted to put himself through this again.

I told Beth that I wasn't convinced he'd quit cold turkey. I thought he'd continue to rationalize his drinking and decide when and what it was okay to have. But she reminded me of something pretty powerful. Now that his disease was going to be out in the open, he'd be judged every time he took a sip. So even if he did think it was fine for him to have a beer or two, others would question it. He'd get the side-eye, the whispers. The dynamic of all of it would change from here on out.

Jeff made it through those first three days and was back to a functioning human being. We talked about getting to an AA meeting. He was nervous to go, and I assured him I'd go with him as long as he needed. Continuing my control/planning/organizational tendencies, I made him a poster board with a calendar so he could tick off his days—celebrating sober milestones, like thirty days and sixty days.

In actuality, all that did was remind him that he was never drinking again. It made each day seem like an eternity and he didn't want to celebrate anything. It just reminded him how much he wanted to drink. There's a reason you always hear "one day at a time" and only focus on what's right in front of you. If you're trying to abstain from drinking, it's really freaking hard. And thinking that you'll never have a beer at a tailgate or on the beach again sucks.

I started cleaning the man-cave after Jeff was finally up and about again and found a tear in the back of the couch. Whiskey bottles.

Probably half a dozen of them were hidden inside the fabric of our couch! I was baffled. And furious. And curious. I started hunting around the room while Jeff was gone. There were smaller bottles tucked in the couch cushions. Empties stuffed in duffle bags and behind winter coats in the extra closet. I couldn't believe what had been happening right under my nose.

He had his first slip up after being sober for six days. Just a little beer. His 'just one' was a giant Fosters can that he'd grabbed from the convenience store down the street.

"It's not a big deal. I just bought it as a reward for when I make it thirty days."

"But you haven't made it thirty days," I said, confused and frustrated.

"I know. It was just the one. It's not like I used to be." As if he was suddenly a new person and had purged the old Jeff and flushed his disease down the toilet.

We went to two AA meetings together, and I think they impacted me far more than they affected him. I was in awe of the men and women there. The ones sharing their stories. What they'd lost. What they'd learned. How proud they were of each chip earned, and just how hard each day was. The strength of a recovering alcoholic is one of the most impressive things I've witnessed. When you meet someone who says they're a recovering alcoholic, you don't really see the full picture. I find them to be so open of their situation, so honest and without shame. What I heard inside an AA meeting gave me an entirely new viewpoint of their strength, struggles, and commitment.

The first AA meeting we attended was at a church near our house. I never grew up religious, but now with two kids, I wanted to get them baptized and start trying out the "church thing." I didn't know that churches require you to be a member to be baptized, so that intimidated me and I wasn't sure where to start. But when I walked into *this* church, I felt immediately at home. We walked in through the children's ward, and I knew it was something Peyton would enjoy. And it was big enough that I could hide in the back of the sanctuary and hopefully not feel so out of place.

The first time the kids and I went happened to be Palm Sunday. Jeff was back to drinking, and we were struggling. I'd given him an ultimatum—three strikes and you're out of the house. I wasn't sure we'd make it, and it was getting close to needing to kick him out. It was as if having the addiction out in the open gave him free reign to drink the way he really wanted to.

When I told him he was getting kicked out, his parents wanted him to go to rehab instead. I didn't trust them to find something or consider how insurance would factor in, so I did the research myself—which was infuriating since I knew he wasn't ready for rehab. But he went. And he stayed there for four whole weeks.

The few days before he left for rehab, I was a complete mess. I had all of our important things—documents, access to money, pills—locked in my car and was sleeping with the keys under my pillow, my hand gripping them and leaving marks on my palm.

It was the most restless and anxious time I can remember. He couldn't be trusted with anything.

The morning before Jeff left for rehab, he and I went for a walk around the neighborhood with the kids in tow. From someone's window, we just looked like a sweet young family, pushing our little ones in a red wagon, talking about the weekend ahead and our big plans. They couldn't see the tears streaming down our faces as we talked about what was happening.

He visited with our neighbors before his dad came to get him, and they later told me that Jeff seemed so dejected. They had given him a double shot of bourbon—where Jeff assured our friends it would be his last "for a while."

At this point, I was so filled with hope—that this would help him, and we could save our marriage. This secret life was no longer private, and our friends and family knew what was happening. We had so much support behind us at this point, and I still wasn't ready to accept defeat and consider divorce. The time away would get him on the right foot. That was my hope.

Jeff's dad came and drove him four hours to the rehab center.

That month was so unbearably hard on Peyton. At only three years old, she just missed her daddy. Every night she'd cry endlessly, since bedtime had been Jeff's domain. For most of his time in rehab, we arranged for him to call her at bedtime so she could hear his voice, but it didn't do much to console her.

Ryan, on the other hand, was my solace. He helped get me through that month. At ten months old, he was so happy and loving and clueless. We'd snuggle at night, and I'd sing to him, and I'd just rock him and cry. He felt so good. And he learned so much that month too—pulling himself up, clapping, and blowing kisses. He was just so sweet and exuded happiness.

Every weekend that Jeff was away, I drove up to see him. I kept it together during rehab because I was full of hope. If you can stay sober for twenty-eight days, isn't that the hump? It was obvious I couldn't understand the addict mindset yet.

The night before I picked him up, we were on the phone, talking about his first weekend home.

"Have you lined up which AA meetings you'll be attending when you get home?" I asked.

"I'm going to take the weekend off and start next week," he said nonchalantly.

My heart SANK. In that moment, I knew he was going to fail. All those weekends when I'd visit, there were family sessions I attended that helped me understand more about addiction. And one of the main things they taught was to have a solid plan for leaving rehab. Know exactly what meetings you're attending and go to one the first day you're home.

I left a message with his counselor, and she called me back late that night, long after the kids were in bed. I sobbed as I relayed my conversation to her. And she could offer no comfort. She also wouldn't admit that she'd been fooled by him too.

During his month there, he was a star student. His counselors were so impressed with him—he was leading AA meetings, mentoring new guys that came in. Jeff even talked about how maybe this was something he could do as a career. It made me even more hopeful. And in that final phone call with Jeff, it all vanished.

I brought him home on the Friday of Memorial Day weekend, and our neighborhood pool opened the next day. We walked down with the kids in the wagon, but I'd forgotten Ryan's float. Jeff offered to go back to the house—just one block away—to get it. And he was gone for forty-five minutes. I later found out that he'd asked one of our neighbors, who didn't know why he'd been away for thirty days, if she had any beer. And she gave him two.

He kept his drinking under wraps for a few days before I caught on. By Wednesday, it was obvious he was back to his old ways, but my deal was I had to prove he was drinking. We were encouraged not to dig around and make the alcoholic feel like they were being watched. That Wednesday was the first night I allowed myself an evening at Al Anon, the support group for those who have relationships with alcoholics, and I trusted him to pick up both kids from day care. I got home at bedtime, and he admitted that he drove Peyton (*three years old, remember!*) home without a car seat. He said he only told me because he knew she'd rat him out. I couldn't even look at him, sitting there in the chair barely keeping his eyes open. I told him to get upstairs and in bed. He was snoring before I had either kid asleep.

All I could think was how devastated I was. How could he do this to me? To his kids? How could he give up his entire life? I had known I was going to be firm on my zero-tolerance policy, but I had NO clue he'd last just a few days. I was so disappointed in him. So sad for my future. And most importantly, so sad for my amazing kids.

Over the years when I questioned my relationship with him, I knew it was worth it because he was more often fun than he was mean. He was entertaining. And he was good at doing the things I wasn't. And most importantly, it was worth it because I didn't believe in divorce. I truly believed in two parent households. I stayed so strong while he was in rehab because I was in a stage of hope. He'd hurt me so badly leading up to that point, but I could have forgiven it all if he came back to me strong, sober, and my old Jeff. The one from when we were dating, from before his cousin died.

The next night when I got home from work, he was screaming and belligerent. I don't even remember why. I was sitting at the table with the kids eating dinner and feeding Ryan his strawberry yogurt.

I calmly told Jeff he needed to go to bed or leave. He chose to leave, and this is the moment that really defined our entire future and custody agreement.

I didn't have the sense three years prior to call 9-1-1 when he was chasing me with a two-week-old baby, but in this particular moment, my first instinct was to grab the phone and call the cops.

I don't even remember what I was planning to call them for, but when I got the phone, Jeff started to chase after me to stop me from calling. Abandoning all desire to keep this hidden, I literally ran out of my house and tried to make it to our friends' house across the street. I got halfway up their driveway when he caught up to me and grabbed me by my ponytail, yanking the phone from my hand and throwing it in our yard. Then he got in his car and peeled out.

I got another phone (we still had house phones, crazy) and dialed 911. I told them that my husband had just left and was drunk and on the road. I was out of breath and clearly upset. After telling her what happened, the operator asked if he'd touched me. I paused for what felt like a solid minute. I knew the answer to this question was significant and I didn't know if I wanted it to be.

But I answered, "Yes. He pulled me by my hair."

She sent police, and I brought Peyton across the street to our friends so she wouldn't be there to see police cars and officers. It was *mortifying* having two cop cars in front of my house. I worked so hard to keep this secret so I wouldn't be the crazy neighbor for people to gossip about, and now that was all out the window.

I relayed to them what happened, and they called in an emergency protective order for me so he couldn't come home. Never having interacted with the cops for more than a speeding ticket, I didn't even know what that was. An emergency protective order is done through the magistrate and lasts for seventy-two hours. After that, I was able to go to the courthouse and request a two week extension while they set a court date to determine if it should be extended. The purpose is to protect someone during a situation where they may be in danger.

I was impressed that the officers initiated this for me, as it wouldn't have been something I would have known about or thought to do. I honestly wasn't afraid of Jeff or in fear of my life, but he was certainly unhinged and unpredictable, and I appreciated the cops being proactive on my behalf. So often, I feel like women aren't proactively protected, and that's when bad things happen.

By the time the cops arrived, I'd received alerts from my bank as to where Jeff had gone. First to Kroger to buy a case of beer, and then he tried to check in to our nearest hotel *for a month*. A whole month. Not at a motel that you'd rent by the week, but a regular Holiday Inn at $120 a night! But he only had access to a debit account that had about $1500 in it, so he wasn't able to. I told the cops where he was, and they went over there after we finished. Unfortunately, the warrant he was being served wasn't one where they could force him to open the door, so he just didn't answer.

After the cops left, I went to get Peyton, and even though it was way past her bedtime by that point, my neighbors put her in front of their tv, turned on a movie, and we all drank a bottle of wine, digesting what just happened. Ironic, but needed. Ryan hadn't left my arms the whole night.

The next morning, I put myself together and went to work like the world wasn't falling apart. I stepped into an unused conference room and called the hotel to let them know that they needed to get a new form of payment, since I'd canceled his card.

Our family and friends were trying to get a hold of him, but he wouldn't answer the phone. Thankfully, that poor girl working the desk was able to get him to open the door enough to see that he was alive, and she let him know he needed to vacate or pay another way.

Around lunchtime, Jeff's dad called.

"I'm coming to get him. Can you pack up some things for him and I'll come get them?"

I had a bag of his things packed, but Jeff insisted on coming himself because he wanted to get—wait for it—his Xbox from the house. His dad let me know they were going to be dropping off Jeff's car too, which Jeff would be driving home.

I called the police so they could be there to serve him the protective order. Thankfully, I was able to get home from work in time to meet the officers before Jeff got there. It wasn't the same guys as the night before, so I let them know that it was very likely Jeff would be drunk if they wanted to breathalyze him once he pulled up.

They came in two patrol cars, so they left the house and got on opposite ends of the street in case he tried to run when he saw them.

Jeff saw the cops once he got to the corner and stopped his car. His dad was following behind him.

Jeff got out of his car, furious, and started yelling at his dad, "You set me up? I can't believe you!"

I felt awful that his dad was taking the brunt of Jeff's anger on this one, but he was able to hold his own.

The cops got out to talk to Jeff, and all the while, I'm standing in our front yard watching this unfold while other neighbors trickled outside for the show. I was so embarrassed.

Surprise neighbors! Jeff wasn't really away this last month helping his ailing parents like I told you. He's been in rehab. And it clearly didn't work.

The officers proceeded to give him a field sobriety test, which he passed. But then, he blew a 0.16 BAC.

Double the legal limit, yet he passed the sobriety test. That's how good he'd gotten at drinking and living his life.

They came over to let me know that because he passed the field test, they wouldn't give him a DUI. Instead, he was being charged with drunk in public, and they were going to let him go with his dad.

Only then, Jeff started mouthing off to his dad over the situation.

His dad took a stand and wouldn't let himself be disrespected. "Good luck to you, son. I'm going back home, and you can figure this out."

And he drove an hour and a half back home.

Because there was no one to claim him, the cops took him, and he spent the night in jail. All because he wanted to make sure he got his Xbox.

We all thought Jeff would just be in jail until he sobered up, but it turned out that because he had been charged with assaulting me after pulling my hair the other day, he had to post a bail of $1200. Jeff's brother and I worked really hard to convince his parents not to post it. We hoped this could be the rock bottom we've all been praying for.

That was all on a Friday, exactly one week since I'd picked him up from rehab, and on Monday morning, I had to go down to the courthouse to get my emergency protective order renewed. My temporary order was extended for two weeks, at which time we'd have an actual hearing to determine if it needed to be lengthened.

While I was there, Jeff had to go before the judge too. I had no idea this was happening so it was all kismet that I was there at just the right time. He was on video from jail, and I snuck into the back of the courtroom to witness. The judge somehow identified me as Jeff's wife, and I kept seeing him watch my reactions while Jeff spoke.

He looked horrendous. Clearly suffering from withdrawal symptoms again and telling the judge whatever he thought would get him released. His hands were shaky. His voice wavered, and his words felt so hopeless. He kept interrupting the judge to try to explain the night and tell him all of the things he was going to do to better himself.

"Your Honor, I am at my bottom. I can't go any lower. I am going to work with my sponsor (which he didn't have). I'll go to a shelter and get marriage counseling."

It was a lengthy list. I wondered if it was really his rock bottom.

The judge said, "Look, I can't do anything about your marriage, and who knows if counseling is even an option for you."

This judge, used to guys like this, wasn't going to be fooled by him.

Regardless, there was no more holding him, so a court date was set for the assault charge and he was released. But he was released with nowhere to go. He didn't have a lot of options since he didn't have many friends. Chris, Jeff's brother, was the only person he talked to while he sat in jail.

"I was Jeff's 'best friend' while he was in jail," Chris said, "and no one else could talk to him, but once he was released, he won't even talk to me. I'm not saying anything to him that he wants to hear. He's looking for his enablers."

Chris was more than Jeff deserved. Jeff didn't even realize the love that was out there for him, and how much we all wanted to help him find his way out of this web.

Jeff called our nanny repeatedly the day he was released asking if he could stay with them "just" that night. But she knew better, and even though it killed her to do it, she told him no. He assumed I told her not to take him in.

He was still blaming others and not taking responsibility for himself. For the record, it broke her heart to turn him away. This was breaking all of our hearts. Jeff was *angry* that people weren't helping him. I would have thought he'd be sad and desperate, but he wasn't. Just angry.

He claimed he was having to sleep in his car, but I later found out that his one friend from work, Patrick, took pity on him, and Jeff was sleeping on his couch.

I was shocked and so proud that Jeff's parents stayed strong as long as they did before finally letting him move in with them. I can imagine how hard it would be to tell your child no when they have nothing. How will he eat? Get gas? Get a shower? It's really heartbreaking to think about it all, and it was overwhelming knowing that it was my HUSBAND. How did he get to this level? And how much sooner would he have gotten to this level if I'd been more honest with myself over the years? I knew he was an alcoholic.

I often think about what really went on in rehab. He talked about the people who didn't want to be there and weren't trying to get better—implying he was. Was his disease that bad that he couldn't resist? Or did he really think he didn't have an addiction and having two beers when he came home wasn't a big deal?

I'll never fully understand, and I'll forever fear for my children, that they may have this propensity for addiction too.

Chapter 5

Letting someone else take over

I t was time to get real about my next steps.

I paid a five-thousand dollar retainer for a lawyer. I didn't know anyone who was recently divorced and had no clue how to begin a search for someone. Lord knows I wasn't about to put out a post on our local Moms Facebook page or ask around at work. This was still a secret to those not close to us. Instead, it was my nanny who had a recommendation. A real shark. A bitch. Exactly who you want, she had said.

When I met with Donna, she was very matter of fact about it all and what we needed to do. At times, it was painful to hear her talk about Jeff like a name on a page, like a loser addict, but I knew it was for the best.

I left her office that first day, and despite spending all that money (just to start!), it gave me a huge sense of peace that someone else could be in charge for a while on my behalf. I didn't have to do it. That was a really liberating feeling, and I drove home with my windows down and an actual smile on my face.

The next day, I emailed my paralegal and my lawyer emailed back. My first thought was, "Shit, that just cost me thirty-five dollars."

Then I got two more emails from the paralegal. There goes another thirteen dollars. Then my lawyer said "THEY" will be at court with me on the 16th. Did that mean I'd pay *each* of them their hourly rate? Could I request that only one of them go? Why did I need both? All I could think about was all the ways I wanted and needed to spend that money. I was barely keeping my head above water and wanted to be able to outsource where I could— someone cutting the grass, ordering dinner in.

Thankfully, it wasn't actually that nit-picky, and she didn't charge me for every email at a ten minute increment, and her paralegal didn't actually come to court with her.

A couple of days later, I had to sign a request for custody and visitation so that my lawyer could get the paperwork processed in time for next week's hearing on the protective order. Again, the thoughts in my head were about the cost. And to add insult to injury, they charge me for travel time AND gas. What? How is that even fair? The office is at a minimum, thirty-five minutes from the courthouse, so we're talking over three-hundred dollars just to go to court. That doesn't include the one to two hours they'll spend with me. So a day in court is going to cost me about a thousand dollars. That five-thousand dollar retainer could go really fast if you're in a big battle with your soon-to-be ex.

I think that's one of the things I fear most for couples going through divorce. It's so easy to spend money with your lawyer and end up in an unfortunate financial situation. If you have a true fear for your kids with your ex, by all means, keep fighting. But in a lot of situations, he's just a shitty husband, but he's a competent father. And if the two of you spend half of their college tuition battling for years, how does that help anyone?

In the moment though, I couldn't think of sharing my kids at all, and I'm sure most women feel the exact same way. This hit me even harder at work one day when a new girl started in my office. She was a single mom to a six-year-old and noticed that I didn't have a ring on my finger.

"Are you a single mom?" she asked.

It was the first time someone asked me something like that.

"It's complicated," I said, shutting her down. That was painful. Like, absolutely gut-wrenching. I was totally unprepared.

A day later, she started talking about her weekend and then casually asked, "Do you have your kids this weekend?"

All I could think about was the possibility that there would be times I wouldn't be with my kids. I wouldn't know that they were safe. I was so sad in that moment picturing a future of sharing my kids.

Even worse, very few people at work knew anything was going on in my life. I think I'd have been a hell of a lot less put together if people knew what I had on my plate. It was only out of sheer embarrassment that I was forced to be tough. While I'm grateful for the support from so many, I kind of hated the pity and people always asking if I was okay. Work was the one place I could go and say, "Let's focus on my work."

I was also getting enveloped with love and support from all over outside of work. Everything from gift cards for food (Pizza was the best! So convenient for me.) and gas and offers to just come over and hang out with me. At Peyton's daycare, I won a week of free child care, which was funny because when I turned in my raffle ticket, I thought, "I bet they give this to me just because they feel bad for me." Ding-ding. I'll take what I can get and relish how beautiful it is when people try to help you out where they can.

I have a friend who is incredibly wealthy and had been following my family blog which had recently been documenting all of the crazy things happening in our world. She wanted to do something nice for us, and man did she ever. She got me a maid service! Weekly. For the whole summer. Beyond feeling so grateful, I kept thinking how nice it must be to be rich and do amazing things like that for people when they are low. It was beyond awesome coming home to no dust, clean sheets, a fingerprint-free fridge, and a clean oven. That gift was incredible on so many levels. It gave me back more time with the kids, for myself, and it made me feel better coming home to a clean house and not worry about when I was going to get to all those necessary tasks.

That first summer, I didn't have to cut my grass either. My dad came over every week and did that. By the next spring, I was ready to do it myself and had my neighbor show me the ropes. Now, it's one of my favorite tasks. I find it so relaxing and a great workout.

I kept going to church after Jeff went to rehab. I sat in the back and cried every week, like each sermon was written just for me. I don't know why, but the tears always felt so good to me. I had to be strong about so many things, and church was the moment when it was okay for me to break. I knew this is where I wanted to make my church home, and I attended a baptism class for me and the kids.

It was just me and one other woman who met with the pastor that night. He asked each of us why we were getting baptized/wanting to baptize our kids. I didn't think I'd cry, but I should have known it was inevitable. I couldn't wait for this moment of rebirth for us.

When I walked out, the other woman stopped me and said, "I think you and I were meant to be in that class together tonight.

One of my best friends is going through your exact situation right now. Would it be okay if I introduced you guys?"

Kismet.

A God wink.

Fate.

Her name was Courtney, and I was dying to talk to her and hear her story and how she was surviving. And I hadn't been able to make time to do it. She understood though. When I told her I'd been meaning to call her all week, I added that being a single parent sucks! And she replied that she totally understood. It does suck. On so many levels.

It took us about a week to connect, and then she had an evening free and came over to my house. Courtney shared with me the story about her husband and his alcoholism. Her story was different but totally the same. I think all of ours are.

She was a stay at home mom, so I find her incredibly brave. The stay at home moms who leave are my heroes. The strength and fearlessness and love for your kids that requires. I can't think of anything more brave.

Her husband was still functioning. He worked in sales and traveled a lot. He got fired from his job for misusing his corporate card. He owed his company thousands of dollars. He hadn't been paying their mortgage. It was a very similar story leading up to Jeff's breaking point though. Embarrassing nights out. Lies and more lies.

She said, "He'd lie even if the truth was better," which sounds like the definition of an alcoholic to me.

We talked about how we could probably forgive the alcohol one day, but it's the lying that totally broke everything. How would we ever trust them again?

And in her case, people told her after he was gone about all of the things they saw him do. She was so upset no one ever told her. I, on the other hand, told her how embarrassed I was when the cop cars suddenly appeared two days in a row and the cat was out of the bag.

The morning after she and I met, Courtney texted me to say, "Just when you think it can't get any worse…" she went to her husband's apartment when he was a no-show for taking their son to his baseball game, and a bar whore answered his door.

He was naked in bed.

Crushing. They'd only been separated about a month. I wondered if this was the first time. I'd assume not, but who knows. Courtney was going through hell taking care of the kids, keeping them living their normal lives, and worrying about losing her house and her livelihood, and he was living a bachelor life in an apartment and getting drunk and hooking up with random women. I wondered if Jeff was doing the same. I had no idea where he was.

Chapter 6

Happy birthday, Ryan!

I was listening to some song on the radio on my way home and thought of Jeff. I thought about how much I loved the old Jeff, the healthy Jeff. I was thinking, "Man, what if this really is it for his drinking? What if I divorce him and he never touches a drink again?"

But then the grounded, practical side of me reminded my heart that I *always* gave him the benefit of the doubt and believed in him too much, and that's what led me to the situation I was in. My head knows that with a personality like Jeff, not drinking will never be easy. This bottom he was on right now could keep him sober for a year or two, but there's very little doubt that drinking would be a lifelong struggle for him.

I regularly take myself back to that first Al Anon meeting I went to on the night Jeff drove the kids home while drunk and without Peyton's car seat. The woman who spoke had two small kids and a husband who had been sober for several years. It was the first time she left him alone with them while she traveled for work (across the country!), and he got drunk and got a DUI while they were in the car.

That woman's story still sits with me five years later.

I didn't want to spend the next few years never feeling comfortable leaving my kids alone with him. Plus, HOW DEVASTATING to think you're "in the clear" and then be right back in that horrible moment. I couldn't put myself through that. And if he can't stay sober for life, I couldn't put my kids through it. If he stays sober, well, then they'd get to spend lots of time with him over the years. And everyone will win.

It made my heart hurt so bad to think that I won't grow old with him, and as I learned to let go, I've realized just how much I loved him and how much he meant to me. It took every ounce of my strength to hold on to my convictions and move forward and never take him back.

At this point, it hadn't even been two weeks yet since Jeff was released and I saw him looking so awful on that courtroom video screen. Part of his release involved regular drug and alcohol testing, and if he failed, he would go back to jail.

To my amazement, he passed his first test. Was it just because he was afraid of going back to jail? He always had a huge fear of authority, and I really believe this testing was what kept him sober for thirty days. When July 2nd came and he was no longer tested, would he go back to drinking? Could the fear of losing his kids keep him from drinking?

I was very anxious for the unknown of what would happen at our upcoming custody hearing. How would I feel when I saw him? I wanted to hug him and tell him everything would be okay. But as I pictured and imagined how that would feel in my arms, the comfort was more for me than him. I kept going back to the fear of being alone forever. Every person I saw at work, the first thing I did was look at their hand to see if there was a ring on it. They didn't even have to be attractive. I was just looking to see who was in my club, and who was in the club I was getting kicked out of.

Father's Day was the day before our hearing, and it was a lot more painful than I anticipated. My sweet manager had gorgeous flowers delivered to me on Friday saying that she figured this would be a hard weekend for me. I didn't realize how hard until I was at church and they played a video to open the service that had dads doing all these things with their kids at various life stages, and oh my word, the waterworks. It's the not knowing that really hurts. Would Jeff be there for any of those things? I honestly didn't know.

The sermon was about baptism (ours was the next weekend), and I swear my pastor put some of those words in there just for me.

He said baptism was about a new life, and for me, being baptized later in life, it really was.

He read a quote from Pat Summerall, the former NFL announcer who spent many years as a struggling alcoholic before finding his relationship with God.

"[F]or the first time in my life, I knew what people meant about being 'born again,'" Summerall wrote. *"I had already accepted that Jesus Christ was the Son of God who died for our sins. Now, I felt I was truly part of his family. I felt ecstatic, invigorated, happier, and freer. It felt as though my soul had been washed clean."* (Ellsworth 2013)

What an interesting person to use as his reference. Was it for me? To give me hope that one day Jeff will get better?

He even said that when the pastors meet with adults prior to the baptism, they are usually in tears by the time they get to "What brought you to this point?" Was he for real? Or did he just have me on his mind when he wrote this week's sermon? Maybe I was just imagining all of that, but either way, it spoke to me and made me feel heard and honored.

As if the sermon wasn't enough, I went to pick up Peyton from her class and they'd made "Best Dad Hands Down" t-shirts. UGH. They had Ryan's itty-bitty prints on there too. Daggers to the heart. Peyton was still pretty clueless about where her daddy was, and I'm sure she thought he was coming home, so it was devastating to see that shirt.

Then we were outside playing later that day, and my neighbor's mom asked me how Jeff's Father's Day was going.

"Oh, pretty good, I guess."

I didn't even know how to respond to someone who wasn't up to speed on our soap opera situation.

Father's Day just one year ago, I was having a great time two days before Ryan was born. I'll say it again, I couldn't believe the direction my life had taken.

The next day was the court hearing for the protective order. Would it be extended? I was under the impression from Donna that it wouldn't be. Jeff showed up and looked totally nerdy—all clean-shaven and a haircut. He had on this awful bright blue shirt that looked like uniform, khaki pants that were actually ironed with a crease, and new blue sneakers.

Donna, my lawyer, was talking to him when I arrived. She was trying to get information out of him and get him to agree to extending the protective order instead of having the full hearing. Jeff was "agitated" to use the words of the domestic abuse lady who was assigned to our case.

"I don't have time to deal with that today," she said.

"He's not a bad guy," is what I wanted to say. He's just sick. And sad. And his whole world was falling apart. Mine was too, but I still had everything—except him. He had nothing. How much must he have hated life right then? It made me cry all day long any time I thought about all of this, and I only kept myself sane by reminding myself that this wasn't my fault. It was his, and I was truly looking out for myself and our kids. And the more he lost, hopefully the faster he'd get healthy.

My jaw about hit the floor when we got into the courtroom and Donna said Jeff agreed to a two-YEAR extension on the protective order—the maximum allowed by law. All this time, (a) she'd been telling me it probably wouldn't get extended, and (b) that if it did, it would likely be for six months. So, imagine my surprise at hearing that.

The judge was the same one who saw him on video two weeks earlier and said, "I want to remind you that you don't have to agree to this. You have a constitutional right to see your kids. Now, I also have the right to take that away, but you have the right to state your case. I don't want you to feel like you're backed into a corner."

Jeff was so sad—and so angry—and just replied, "No, I just want to get the ball rolling."

But backed into a corner is *exactly* how Jeff felt right then. Donna said he used those exact words to her outside the courtroom.

I could tell the judge was very concerned about him agreeing to two years without contact with his kids, and he asked me if I was concerned with contact when he was sober. I said no and offered up my mom as the go-between. A guardian ad lidem (GAL) was appointed for the kids. He essentially acts as their lawyer and tells the judge what he feels is in their best interest. The judge almost always listens to what that person recommends and does that. I was told to be as open and available to him as possible and to get him on my side fast.

We left the courtroom, and his dad was sitting there waiting. He said he'd driven down separately, wanting to provide some unwanted support to his son. I gave him a brief hug and then went to get Jeff's things out of my car. I wondered how Jeff felt when he saw the Father's Day things I put in the bag. It broke my heart all weekend, and I wonder what it did to him.

When I'd think about how Ryan, and even Peyton, will never remember sharing a home with their mommy and daddy, it was almost enough to crush my resolve and take him back. Before I knew the extent of his drinking, I used to think about how the pros outweighed the cons. How the good times outweighed the bad. And how much I really did love him. But then I questioned it—is that really true?

Not seeing him or hugging him or talking to him had me romanticizing things. I did love him terribly, but it had been a really long time since I'd been *in love* with him. It had been so long since he'd met my needs and treated me the way I know I deserve. But when I'd think about Jeff being with another woman and bringing her around my kids, I truly couldn't breathe. It's not him being with someone *else*, but it's *who* he would bring around my kids. I couldn't stomach the thought. The place that he was in would never attract a quality woman that I'd be comfortable with.

Because I had to be so *together* during the day, I broke down most nights while writing in my journal. I had to type it all out because my brain moved too fast for my fingers to keep up. Peyton came down while I was in the middle of writing one night, and I was sobbing. She asked me why I was crying, and I told her I was reading a sad story.

I felt bad that Peyton caught me crying. That was the first time, miraculously, that it happened. I'm human and it was bound to, but it's also my job to shelter her as much as I can. And I guess "as much as I can" left a few gaps in there for being human and having a break down.

My life with her was SO hard at this time. At three years old, she couldn't grasp the permanence of what was happening in her life and she constantly acted out. She never wanted to listen to me, and she asked for Jeff a lot. Bedtime was pure torture since that was his special time with her. And I was all alone. Yes, I could have all the help I wanted, but at the end of the day, it was just me. I couldn't rely on my parents or my friends around the clock, so I had to step up and be *the* parent and do the best that I could to take care of them.

I often thank God that Jeff and I survived long enough to bring Ryan into this world, because his sweet, angelic face is sometimes all that got me through when my chest would physically hurt with the pain. Ryan was twelve months old and made me so unbearably happy. I never got a moment to breathe with him because of his age, but he was the light of my life. Of course, I love Peyton just as much and I tried to show her love even *more*, but just as being around negative or depressed people affects you, being around a scared and sad child is heart-wrenching. Ryan didn't know any better, so he was happy as a clam. That energy was infectious, and when I didn't have it, I kind of fell apart.

Our custody hearing was a separate case from the protective order, and it took place two days later—on Ryan's first birthday. If I could isolate all the good moments, it was such a special day, but it was marred with horrible things I never dreamed of experiencing. I made cupcakes and Peyton and I went into Ryan's room with balloons and to play with him and wish him a happy birthday. He was so happy, and we ate cupcakes for breakfast! Peyton was in heaven, and Ryan really enjoyed his first taste of sugar! He licked all of the icing off and then started diving into the cupcake itself.

The amount of time I spent crying before the hearing made me wonder if I was beginning to lose it. I cried when I dropped Peyton off at daycare that morning. It was her teacher's first day back from maternity leave, and we'd been pretty close.

She said that when she got in, administration told her, "You have another custody case in your room," and then they said Peyton's name.

Her teacher said, "That was not the name I was expecting to hear."

I got choked up and did my best to fill her in.

I wondered if this was the day I wouldn't be able to keep it together at work and my secret would be revealed. As had become the norm though, the pile of tears I cried on the way in was enough to get me through the day before I could go home and break again.

When I got to the courthouse, I saw no sign of Jeff, so I went in. At my lawyer's recommendation, my dad came to show that he was on board to offer support. Even though we had a solid arrangement, it still took an hour to get everything done. The judge asked Jeff if he was planning on getting a lawyer, and he said no.

The judge said, "I can't tell you that you have to get one, but this is a complicated system to navigate through and I'm guessing you don't have a lot of experience here. It's in your best interest to get one."

We initially set our hearing for a permanent agreement for late July but then pushed it since Jeff said he wanted to check in to treatment—which never happened.

After court, Jeff had a visit with Ryan while he was at our nanny's house. She said it went really well and Jeff was engaged and "himself" the whole time. Even better, she said she'd be happy to have him over again any time… which was good since she was on the agreement to have him over once a week! He brought the kids some books and read "Guess how much I love you" to Ryan, and she said Jeff started crying.

That weekend, we had Ryan's birthday party and our baptism. Family was turning out in droves to support us—even Jeff's brother and his family came from Kentucky to stay with us. His parents, who were keeping Jeff, chose not to come. I'm sure they were worried about how we'd all judge them and their decision to take Jeff in. Plus, Jeff wasn't allowed to be at the party due to our protective order, so it showed solidarity with him that they stayed home.

The party was perfect. It was the first day of summer, so I did an ocean theme. It was a full house but never overwhelming. I really focused on Ryan and keeping myself busy. I didn't even have a chance to think about Jeff unless someone was asking how things were or if we should be posting pictures to Facebook that he'd see. Ryan did great and posed for some adorable smash cake pictures.

When it was over, I looked back at the photos from Peyton's party, with Jeff and I on either side of her. This time, just me. And that was really tough. Really sad.

It's hard not having a crystal ball. Hard not to know how the next eighteen years would go with my darling children. Would he get his act together and be a parent? Would I be sharing my time with him? Would we always love each other and be able to successfully co-parent as they got older? Could we have one birthday party? Could we all pose for pictures like we're still one big happy family? Is there any circumstance in which we'd BE a big happy family?

But then, my mind would drift back to that woman from Al Anon, and her husband who was two years sober and got a DUI, and he failed them all.

The next day, Peyton, Ryan, and I were all baptized together. Ryan didn't cry, and Peyton behaved and let the pastor put the water on her head which is as much as I could hope! As usual, I broke down during the prayer time. At our church, we use that time to get up and light a candle while music plays. I never had the guts to get up and light a candle, but I always prayed in my seat for Jeff and for Peyton, and I'd always completely break down, the tears streaming down my face while my eyes remained closed. My cousin was sitting next to me and started crying even harder than me. There's so much love out there and so much pity for us too. That's hard to face, and it was hard to stomach wondering what people were thinking about when it came to my situation. It's still hard today when people hear my story.

Before my brother-in-law went home, I had a list of chores that I'd purposely left on the fridge but would never have asked him to do while he was here—and he did nearly everything on the list in about thirty minutes. Things that would have taken Jeff weeks. The curtain rod was fixed, car seat switched out, fridge filter replaced, new batteries in the kids' books. I was so grateful.

That endless week wrapped up with my very first bible study— Beth Moore's *David: Seeking a Heart Like His*. I was so new to Jesus and studying the bible, and I was so intimidated to walk into that room with dozens of women who knew way more than me about God!

But bible study today mostly happens through video, so we spent almost an hour watching Beth speak in her hilarious Southern accent, as she explained so many things in layman's terms so I could follow along.

Even on my first night, she spoke to my heart and my current situation—making me yearn for more the following week. She said that a *talkative* person who is full of shame makes an excellent liar. I just kept thinking, "Huh, that's Jeff." Such a great liar. Personable and could talk to walls. And full of shame that he carried around—which only led to more and more drinking over the years.

Chapter 7

Settling into a new routine

It was Jeff's first time seeing Peyton in a full month. The night before, I read her a great book called *The Invisible String* and it was about loving people and them being with you even if they aren't physically there.

At first, she wasn't in to it, but then she made me read it twice. I caught her in a talkative moment and asked her some questions about her daddy.

"Are you sad that daddy doesn't live here anymore?" - No.

"Are you sad that you haven't seen daddy?" - No.

The answers made me feel good that she wasn't getting totally ruined through all of this. She had been talking about seeing Jeff all week though, so I knew she was looking forward to his visit.

She and my mom, who was acting as our go-between, sat on the steps waiting for him that afternoon. Jeff brought flowers. Were they for me? For Peyton? My mom said he just left them on the counter, so who knows what his intent was. We assumed they were for me, as if bringing flowers would get him out of the doghouse or something. *Like it could be that simple.*

They went to the pool and Peyton finally had her daddy to throw her high in the air—something that broke my heart when my brother and sister-in-law, Chris and Beth, were here. Seeing Peyton get jealous watching Chris throw his kids was just another reminder of the things she'll miss out on.

Peyton asked Jeff if he was going to sleep over, and my mom said, "No, he sleeps at his house."

And Jeff replied, "Well kinda."

I mean, come on. Let's keep it basic for her. This isn't about you and how uncomfortable you are. I left him a note with the phrases I use and what I tell her. But he did everything his own way without regard for others, so I'm sure that list went right onto his passenger seat never to be seen again.

That night when I put her to bed, I could still hear whimpers from her room almost an hour later, so I broke down and opened the door. She told me she missed her daddy and wanted a sleepover with him. She asked about going in his car and if I'd put a car seat in there.

"Is your bed daddy's bed too?" she asked.

"No. It's just mommy's bed now. Daddy has his own bed."

It was so hard for her, and she was so sad and confused.

I really wanted to talk to Jeff and understand what was going on in his head. He was clearly romanticizing the same way I was, and obviously, with everything lost to him, he was sad and desperate. He wrote on Facebook a post that left no one to wonder what may or may not be going on with our relationship.

another lonely night

I miss you. Asking what you want for dinner, seeing your smile, waking up next to you, kissing me on the shoulder. You next to me in the car. Calling you to see how your day was. God i miss you. —🙁 feeling alone.

I could have asked him to delete it, but why not let him have the outlet? Honestly, it made me feel good too to read it—which is exactly why I was okay keeping the protective order in place. It would just make me weak if I talked to him. I reminded myself how hard this was to do with Peyton at only three years old. I couldn't imagine doing this to her or Ryan at five or seven or nine. No way. I couldn't do it.

Shortly after, Jeff was preparing to go to rehab again. One night, he was having dinner with Peyton and I had prepped what I wanted him to say to describe his absence. I'd read a good explanation that basically said, "Daddy is having some grown up problems so he has to go take care of them to get better. Being a grown up can be hard sometimes… I love you very much and will see you soon."

He never shared that with her.

Later that night, Chris called me to make sure he wasn't confused and that we were on the same page… because Jeff told him that he had to go to treatment for three months and then he could come back home. This obviously never came out of my mouth, but it was hard to balance giving him hope and also helping him understand reality. He still treated the situation as if he was going through all of this to "do his time" and then come back home and have me back. That's not reality, and he had to learn to live on his own and be a functioning member of society. I asked Chris to set him straight without mentioning divorce.

It was incredibly disappointing to hear that he thought he could just "do his time" and then come home like it never happened. He had torn my world upside down. On one side of the coin, he'd tell people that he feels so hopeless and he doesn't want to think that seven years of marriage is flushed down the toilet because of what he's done. And yet, he still wouldn't face reality or want to get better for himself.

It just reminded me again how strong people in AA actually are. What a step to commit to making your life better! It's a huge deal. It's not what Jeff did. My mom got it right when she said, "He did his thirty days' time, came home and drank. Now he wants to do his ninety days and come home again."

I laughed with her when I had the realization of how clever he was when it came to drinking. All the tricks he used on me. One reason it was so easy to believe that his behavior was due to medication, not alcohol, was because he would open a beer in the evening and take two sips and seem to never touch it again. I used to get ANGRY that he'd open it and only have two sips. Now I realize that was all part of his show—"Look, Ashley—I don't drink. I can barely finish one beer."

HA! Then unbeknownst to me, he was upstairs with his hidden alcohol—waiting to be alone so he could pull back the fabric of the couch and pull out his cheap bourbon and pour it into another unsuspecting container. So sneaky. Too bad he couldn't put that effort into work or his family or chores.

At the end of the day, no matter how healthy he got, I could never be with him simply because I'd live my whole life in fear. I'd always wonder if he was lying. Always wonder if he was going to break my heart again. Always wonder how it would impact the kids the next time.

Around this time, I was introduced to Glennon Doyle's book *Carry On, Warrior*. Glennon is a long-time recovering alcoholic. She was one of my biggest influences over the next year because I could feel her emotions to my core, and she shared her story with so much humor and heartbreak. I know it wouldn't have made any difference because Jeff **needed** a bottom, but I can't help but wonder if this book would have made a difference to him. I know the answer is no, because he never would have read it. He would have pretended to read it.

Since Jeff couldn't talk to me and didn't *want* to talk to my mom, he resorted to my friends and our nanny. When he talked to my friend Katie, she'd say he sounded sincere and genuine.

He told her, "I had a moment while sitting on the floor of the jail cell when I thought about how crazy it was that I couldn't wait to get home to have a drink. I thought about Ashley downstairs and how I should be down there with her watching a movie but instead I was upstairs shoving a bottle of something down my throat. I couldn't believe how this addiction was ruling me."

I never heard him speak that way to anyone, so that made me believe he was being honest that jail was his bottom (or he wanted it to be).

Okay, so if now he's trying to climb the hill back up, what's to say that he's not going to fall before reaching the top, or worse, get to the top and only realize there are more hills and valleys in front of him, and his addiction isn't beat? How long would he be recovering before he'd be back to being ruled by addiction?

These are the unknowns I had to keep in my head when I'd think about how different life could be if he was to get clean and sober and motivated and loving again. I fear I'd take him back in a heartbeat, and that just felt wrong to me.

Glennon talks about God sending partners to us to help us heal—but the healing part is hard. And sometimes one or both partners can't take it, so someone bails, or makes it impossible for the other partner to keep on loving. She says that God keeps sending us these healing partners in different forms (family, friend, dog, etc.) until one sticks. (Doyle, 2014)

But I was confused with that message.

Was *I* the one who was supposed to help Jeff heal?

Was it supposed to be mutual healing?

It didn't feel like he was healing anything in me, just breaking me. Just forcing me to find someone to help heal me—which, in my case, felt like God or the church, or maybe even Courtney, who was facing her own single mom battles. Was she sent to me to help me get through all of this? Was I sent to help her too?

If I'm the one who was meant to help Jeff heal—is that what I was doing by setting him free and forcing this rock bottom on him? Or is that only part one and THEN I'm supposed to let him back in our lives when he "sees the light"? I had no clue.

A few days later, I was lying in bed still reading *Carry On, Warrior* and I just LOST it. My tears and sadness were so intense that I needed to pull out the computer to take myself out of it and clear the thoughts from my mind. I'd been reading a chapter about her and her husband not being able to afford their home, and they needed to move and rent. She talked about the freedom they felt not being burdened by money and how happy they were. How happy THEY were. Sure, it's a lot easier to do hard things when you do them together. That's one of the themes of her book— we can do hard things. When I read that, I heard in my head, TOGETHER. Together, we can do hard things. As in, with my partner, I can do it. I know that's not what she was trying to convey and she'd be pissed to know that was my temporary interpretation, but in that moment, that's how I felt. *Together* meant me and my partner, but now I know it means my tribe. It means all of those that rally for me, love me, and guide me through life's highs and lows.

Thinking about the whole 'together' thing always makes me wallow on the single mom aspect of all this. One of my biggest fears was having to move because I couldn't afford the house on my own. It may seem like my worries should have been elsewhere, and they were. But the house. Our home. It's the safety net. It's where we can just *be*. And it's all the kids knew. It was the one thing that wasn't changing for them. Peyton still had her room, her toys, her swing set, and neighbors. I thought about all the work that I'd done to make this place my forever home. Then, I pictured my kids growing up in another place with no yard, and that was it. Heart break. Constant heart break.

I knew that if I ever remarried, I'd probably have to move and find a new home to start our newly joined life, but I also kind of knew that in my heart, it'd probably be me on my own as a single mom for a looooong time. That was utterly depressing to me. I couldn't stomach that I was going to raise my kids as a single mom. It broke my heart into a million pieces, and I couldn't get the words out without painful cries escaping. This was not what I signed up for, and it's not what any child should have to be raised with. I was so prepared to spend my entire life not in love and just existing in my marriage because I *like* Jeff a lot and because he's my babies' daddy and they deserve a great one. And if he could have been that for them, I would have done that for them.

I was heartbroken. I was heartbroken over the family that I was never going to have and that my kids were never going to know.

But I didn't miss him. At all. I missed everything about the life that should include him, but the actual person—I hated him. I struggled daily wondering if I should be seeing him through the good times and the bad, or if I got a free pass because it's an addiction we're dealing with. It's not just fighting or an affair or some other excuse for "giving up" on marriage. Yet, that's still totally how I felt. And I know I should feel okay with what I was doing—proud even. But I didn't. Well, I did, but I didn't. It made my heart ache just thinking about it. Family vacations? There's no such thing. Our family was incomplete now. I didn't even know how long it would take to feel comfortable traveling with both of them on my own. Disney? I could never do that by myself. The beach? How do you watch two little kids in the ocean when I don't even like going in the water?

Now that my kids are older, I can say that there's a way to make those vacations work. I know better now. My parents came with me to Disney the first time, and we brought Courtney and her kids to the beach with us that first summer. My friend Kristin came the year after that. And my parents were a constant presence.

Always there to help with shuttling the kids where they needed to be and being the additional support we all needed—whether that was at a swim meet or a school performance. My friends who had to move post-divorce are thriving now, and so are their kids. Even those who don't have family nearby. The tribe. That's how it happens.

Chapter 8

Protecting the assets

Apparently, I don't have the best judgement. When I was eleven, I liked Tonya Harding and thought for sure she was innocent. Now, she does shit like celebrity boxing. When I was in the 5th grade and watched the white Bronco speeding down the highway, I didn't think OJ was a murderer.

"Why would he do that?" I thought.

I wanted to believe the best in people and did not know how cruel the world was.

As an adult, I still pretty much saw the world that way. For years, I hid myself from the truth in front of me because I wanted to believe everything Jeff told me—about his anxiety, about giving up his liquor, about drinking less than one beer. It hurts that I almost let him break that good spirit in me, and for that alone, I knew I could never be with him again.

Even though I knew I couldn't be with him again, in the back of my mind, I was always left wondering, "But Ashley, WHAT IF he never takes a drink again? What if you ruin your kids' chances of having a two-parent household because you're stubborn?"

What kind of shit is that? And how horrible to let myself think that I am STUBBORN (*I am*) for choosing to leave him. And let's be honest, every day he would want to drink. He may very well take things one day at a time and each day keep succeeding, but until he could get himself some intense therapy, he'd never be well. I think it would have been years before he even reached the 8th step (Anonymous 1981) and could apologize for all of the horrors he himself has brought upon me and our kids.

Even still, how did I keep my resolve through everything? Having the protective order really saved me in all of this, and I know that's not something that a lot of women have the 'luxury' of having as they go through a divorce. If I'd been communicating with him, we may have gotten along or maybe we would have fought. He may have broken sobriety sooner. I have no idea, but I hypothesized that dinner once a week would turn in to spending all day Saturday at the house. And then it would be picking someone up from daycare, and it would feel like we were still us. Still broken. Still sad. Still uneven.

I desperately needed to hold on to the fantasy of a GOOD and THOUGHTFUL and HARDWORKING man who could love me and my kids, because if I didn't, I'd for sure lose it. I'd been surviving on fumes for eighty-one days at that point. It felt like forever, but in reality—it was nothing. I had so much work ahead of me. So much exhaustion, and so much strength to find.

But I knew I could do it, and I knew I could make it on my own. The problem now is that I knew how *awful* and *hard* it was to be a single parent, and I just didn't want to do it. But I had to be strong because it was the right thing for all of us.

I hadn't even made it through the summer, and it felt like life was completely overwhelming and out of control. Jeff said he hadn't had a drink since jail on May 30th. Was that true? I don't know. I almost hoped not. It would make me feel more confident in my decision. I *wanted* him to keep falling off the wagon—to prove me right! How horrible is that?

Jeff was getting really antsy wondering if there was any hope for us, so I needed to strike fast to get him to sign our property settlement agreement (PSA). For those who have never been through a divorce, a property settlement is your key paperwork that says everything from who gets the house to how you're splitting your 401K to what the specific custody details will look like. Before Jeff had the sense to lawyer up, I wanted him to sign those papers. Not because I wanted to be vindictive, but because he'd already drained us so much financially, and I wanted to cut monetary ties with him as fast as possible.

I'm a saver. I shop a lot too, but only after I've contributed diligently to my retirement and savings accounts. So, over our seven years together, I'd put away a lot into my retirement. My dad is a financial planner, so I knew to start saving early to let it just sit and multiply as I got older. It made me sick to have to give that up. But in most states, even when one person is clearly at fault, it's hard to keep any more than sixty percent of your assets. I was afraid that when he saw all of that 401K money that he'd want it—or more specifically that his dad would see it and push for it. And that's exactly what happened. They paid for him to have a lawyer. And since it was Jeff, the story his lawyer got was far from the truth, so what she thought she was advocating for was just never going to happen.

At this point, I think he was still sober—or at least, trying to be. I stalked him in countless ways to try and get a sense of where his head was and how sobriety may or may not be going, but without seeing him and talking to him, it was a lot harder.

That's why, when I was awoken late at night by a phone call from some guy who he knew from rehab, I let him talk. I was craving information.

"Jeff is in a bad place, on the edge of a drink all the time. He's all 'woe is me' and down on himself, and he wants to know if he has a chance to get you back."

This stranger continued, "Jeff is obsessed with knowing what is going on in your life (*Ditto!*). Wondering if you're with another guy (*Like I had the time*) or moving on."

I spent most of the call just listening, and we were on the phone for fifty-five minutes. I needed to hear confirmation that Jeff was not recovering and not taking accountability and really, not at rock bottom yet.

I stayed on the phone because it was validation that what I was doing was the right thing. He also kept saying, "I don't even think I'm going to tell Jeff that we talked."

We hung up at 11:58PM and the Verizon bill shows he called Jeff at 12:03AM—and they talked for forty-four minutes.

The following week was our court hearing to discuss custody and child support. Our guardian ad lidem (GAL) was involved, and I felt good about how things would go. Jeff hadn't gone to rehab as we'd discussed. He barely had a job. Was living at home with his parents—and we could both agree we'd never let the kids stay there overnight because they smoked. For the short term, I had no concerns about the safety of the kids or the court allowing them to stay in my care one hundred percent of the time.

But I was still so concerned how it would turn out. How shameful and sad to turn your kids over to the courts. That's what I'd done. Yes, Jeff caused it, but I *did* it. It sucked.

Court was unbearably awkward, and Jeff was in a simply jubilant mood. It was odd—and off—and made me feel like he'd taken a few shots before getting to court to settle his nerves. He rambled on and on when the judge would ask a question and never really made any sense.

Judge: "Do you think you'll be able to get a job making $45,000?"

Jeff: "I could never make that much. That's A LOT of money. I never saw my pay-checks. Ashley did all of the bills and stuff."

(For the record, Jeff did make that much at his last job which is why that's what his payments were to be based on.)

Once we settled at a temporary child support amount, the judge asked about using our joint account to deposit money.

Jeff said, in a smug tone to suggest I had done something wrong, "Well it's funny, I went to use my debit card and it was declined. I don't have access to the joint account."

The judge simply replied, "Well, I think that's what any reasonable person would have done."

Did Jeff forget that in his drunken craze on May 29th that he tried to book a month at a Holiday Inn? Yes, any reasonable person would have canceled his card and taken out all of the money to keep him from destroying his family.

I spoke to the GAL about Jeff's behavior in court, and he said, "Can I tell you something? I thought the same thing [about him being inebriated], but I didn't know him enough to know if that was just his personality."

When I told him, no, that definitely wasn't normal. He said, "Damn, I wish I'd known. I would have had him breathalyzed right then."

Oh, I was so mad at my lawyer. Why didn't she tell me this was something that gets done? We could have done it day one when we went back in June. We could have done it in August. What a mess. And now I'll never know if he was drinking before court those days.

After the hearing I spent a lot of time talking to Jeff's dad (while my dad talked to Jeff... so awkward). He said that they were "about tapped out if Jeff didn't get a job tomorrow."

My question always was WHY was Jeff so expensive? I know he was expensive out of the gate because they were shortsighted and paid for him to be in a motel for more than two weeks, so I'm sure that was a huge chunk of change. But then it should have just been gas and food after that. I would hope they weren't dumb enough to give him spending money—because there's nothing he needed to be buying except dinner on the rare times he went out with Peyton.

I told him that as soon as Jeff signed the property settlement that I'd be able to write him a check for $10,000, but he didn't take the bait.

———◆———

A few days later, I woke up to some urgent texts from my mom because Jeff called her at midnight. He appeared to have been his usual drunk self and was agitated, aggressive, and generally made no sense. She was on the phone for an hour with him complaining about the PSA and how he deserved $125,000 from me, how he is going to get custody of his kids, and on and on. Just a general mess.

Obviously hearing all of this confirmed my gut instinct, and I felt proud of myself for trusting it for once. That day, Jeff went to Peyton's daycare to have lunch, and the toughest part is that the visit was great. Her teacher said that the visit was adorable. He was engaging with her and she had a blast.

Once it was time to come in for nap, she started crying and he rubbed her back—and then *he* started crying. One of the older assistants came over and sat with her while Jeff was there. After Jeff left, Peyton cried for another ten minutes. Her teacher rocked her and said it caught her off guard how emotional SHE got. For anyone involved, even on the periphery, it was just so heartbreaking to watch someone fall apart, and it was so obvious he loved his kids, and he could be a great dad. That's the horrible part. He was just throwing it all away.

All that said, I know this teacher dreaded me coming in to pick up Peyton that day and having to tell me all this. She started so positive with how great the visit was… then she got to the "but."

"Wellllll, I don't know for sure since I didn't experience it, but Miss K said she smelled alcohol on him before he left."

Great. Bless her heart.

Then she said, "But they were outside and so sweaty. It could have just been in his pores from last night."

Okay, even so. This was someone who was supposedly ninety days sober.

Next, I picked up Ryan, who at this point was still with our nanny and not at the same daycare. Jeff showed up there after his lunch with Peyton, and my nanny said he was an emotional wreck. He came in and just put his head on her shoulder and cried and cried. Eventually she got him to calm down, but she said that was the worst ever.

"I almost offered him a drink just to calm him down," she joked.

Great, again. Then once he was calm, he had a great visit with Ryan too. Great dad, bad alcoholic. My nanny finally admitted that she thought she caught a whiff of alcohol too when he was leaving.

His brother Chris tried to remind me not to focus on speculation and only on fact. But let's be real. That's how we got into this mess. I knew in my gut what was going on, but until I caught him at 7AM pouring whiskey into his Diet Coke, I didn't KNOW. Is that really what I wanted to wait for? It's hard to catch a manipulative alcoholic like him. He put all his energy in to hiding it.

I decided to make an extremely uncomfortable call to his parents to let them know I felt like he was drinking. They didn't believe me, I could tell.

"We don't have any alcohol in the house," they said.

Right, and your son doesn't drive around all day long doing God knows what. Get with it. Pay attention.

After that incident, he went radio silent for a few days, and I was worried. Would I always feel this way? Would I always wonder if he was drinking? Did I hope that he *was* drinking?

That night I rocked Ryan to bed and just cried and loved on him and didn't want to let him go. Peyton didn't really let me love on her like that anymore, so Ryan was my comfort. So innocent. So loving. It breaks my heart that he hadn't had a dad in his life—not like he should.

Chapter 9

Navigating

The first birthday I had to celebrate on my own was Ryan's first birthday. His was such a whirlwind because our lives had *just* been rocked and I didn't have time to step back and think about all of it. And I had more support than I could accept.

But a few months later, it was time for Peyton's birthday. I had her party at a local gymnastics place, and this was her first legit party with actual friends from daycare and not just family.

It was wonderful, overwhelming, and devastating all at the same time. She was in her element as the center of attention and had such a great time! It was hot and sweaty in there, and I immediately regretted not providing more for the parents. Thankfully I had brought waters and had that as an option. (Now I totally know better and have adult beverages whenever allowed!)

My poor cousin came to the party and ended up babysitting Ryan the entire time, which wasn't my intention. But I underestimated how much I'd want to be on the floor with Peyton and soaking in her happiness and taking in some of that for myself. Ryan was not content sitting in the stroller and spent most of the party roaming the floor with my mom or cousin not far behind.

I was having a great time and not even thinking about Jeff until the end of the activity portion. The kids were using the parachute and Peyton was in the center getting to jump around. Then the party leader said, "Do Mom and Dad want to join in?"

In I went and we had a blast, but it was a painful reminder, and it was poor form on the gym's part because they should have asked who was in attendance. With so many family types these days, it was hardly safe for her to assume there was a "Mom and Dad" who would join in.

Next, we opened presents. It was the first and last time I ever had kids open presents at a party. The kids were SWARMING and I couldn't get them under control. One boy's dad quickly became my hero and used his "dad voice" to get everyone to back down and sit their butts on the ground. It lasted about twelve seconds, but it was so heroic and devastating and heartbreaking.

And I just thought, "Wow, look at all of these dads here." And not just there, but participating and engaging with the kids. It was beautiful. And Jeff could be like that. He was a great dad and so good at playing. But instead, we'd reached a point where he wasn't even aware that she was having a birthday party.

Peyton didn't show any signs of missing her dad or being anything less than elated all day, so that's wonderful. She did have her mini "I want my daddy" cry at bedtime when she didn't want to go, and I was forcing her. I never knew how to respond to that because I didn't understand what she was trying to convey. Was she doing it because she knows it makes me pity her? Was she truly conveying the emotion? I didn't know, so I just tried to downplay it and giggle with her as much as I could.

As a kick in the gut, I had asked my father-in-law to make a doll cradle for Peyton's birthday. He's really handy and into woodwork, so I thought it would be something special that he and Jeff could do together. Instead, they bought her a shitty, piece of crap cradle from the store. It was so cheap that I had to return it and pick out something else.

———————◆———————

A few weeks after Peyton's birthday, I was doing something that most sane soon-to-be divorced women would never do—I went on a beach vacation with my ex's family, without my ex. I was literally going on a trip with Jeff's family, and he was not invited. I was completely dreading the trip, but I wanted to do what was right for the kids.

They would love being with their cousins, and I wanted to give them that chance. I honestly didn't know how involved we'd be with them in the future, and while I can bring them that joy, I wanted to. But I was dreading it. I hated his parents at the time and blamed them for so much. Not that that's fair either, but it was true. They raised Jeff with no life management skills and never had him take on any responsibility, and at thirty-five, he'd fallen apart.

My sister-in-law, Beth, called me shortly before the trip. I'd been wanting to talk to her since I'd seen on the phone records that she talked to Jeff for over thirty minutes one night, but I didn't want to outright ask her about it. She's so diplomatic and it's not her style to gossip in that way. I don't even know how our conversation got going, but I know I sobbed through most of it.

It helped Beth understand my hesitation for the beach and also realize why I was struggling so much not talking to Jeff. This Pollyanna view I'd held onto fell apart more and more every day, and I didn't know if any of the future happiness I envisioned for Jeff and I would ever come to fruition. I wasn't hoping that we'd be together, but I wanted us to co-parent and be good friends down the road.

All Beth would admit of her conversation with Jeff is that he was no longer going to meetings or working the steps. He swore he wasn't drinking, though. Of course, right there he lost all credibility in my eyes since sweet Miss K from the daycare said she smelled it on him. And our nanny did too.

Two days before leaving, Chris called me and said, "Hey, I just wanted to see if you had any questions about anything."

"Umm, no. Am I supposed to?"

"Well, no. My parents want you to know that they don't have any animosity towards you and it's just the situation."

He went on with a whole spiel that I'm sure he spent time crafting, and I simply replied, "Well, that's all fine, but I do have animosity. I'm very disappointed and angry and I have no intention of talking to them while I'm there."

He was totally not prepared for that response, poor guy. But I'm glad I was honest. I'm not sure what of that he shared with his parents, but they kept their distance and I bet I didn't have to be around them for more than an hour and a half during the two days I was there.

When we got to the beach, the kids and I had all afternoon to ourselves before everyone arrived. Despite the strangeness of the situation, it was great to see Chris and Beth and the kids. I adore them.

Peyton followed her cousin around like a puppy dog, and it was adorable and annoying. But what did work in my favor is that her cousin didn't wear a diaper at night anymore, and Peyton was dry both nights we were there—and then the next two nights at home! Incredible. Worth the trip, right there.

My father-in-law was enamored with Ryan, and it was actually sweet watching them walk down by the water. It was the one time I got emotional and disappointed that Jeff's *parents* were the ones getting to share this experience with our children and not him. It hurt a lot and made me so sad for Jeff.

I joked with Chris how shocked I was that his parents left Jeff home alone since we weren't even allowed a key to their house our whole marriage, and then Chris bomb-shelled on me that his parents put him up in a hotel for the week. WHAT? I don't know what's worse. I guess in their mind, they didn't want him to burn down the house or steal things, so they might as well pay to put him in a hotel for the week. But how pathetic and soul crushing for him. Just as bad, his mom wouldn't let him touch her washing machine, so he had to give her his clothes to wash while he lived there.

I told Chris that it sounded like his parents were getting comfy with him there, and he agreed. It seemed like they were planning on this being long-term.

Chapter 10

Learning to heal

I signed up for DivorceCare, a free support group that is held in churches around the country, and I highly recommend it—regardless of your religious beliefs. My church offered it that fall, and I begrudgingly signed up, afraid to see the types of people in the class. I was still so judgmental about divorce.

I learned that during this grief period, emotional energy can take up to eighty-five percent of your overall energy supply, leaving only fifteen percent for physical and spiritual energy. And I absolutely believe that. I was really surprised how hard it was for me to interact with others and how much I craved being on my own. I was tired and needed to be alone to get myself rested.

I continued going through the DivorceCare program, and we'd reached the week focused on the impact on kids. And it couldn't have been more depressing. Divorce affects kids, obviously. It hurts them. It messes them up. Girls lack the male role model to know who they want to marry. Boys lack the male role model to idolize. The point was not to make us feel bad for getting divorced, but to help us realize that it does impact the kids, and we need to know how to navigate that and minimize the negative impact. It was so painful.

I had this hope that going through divorce while the kids were young would make it easier—nothing bad to remember. And suddenly I wasn't convinced that leaving while they were young does all that much to make it better. All it really does is force them to live their full lives without that male figure and be accustomed to that. My dad and brother were really going to have to step up. Or I needed to find another partner. I cried just thinking about it all.

I had a woman from the class over for a playdate that week. Her girls were two and three, so they were right in between my kids. Everyone had fun playing, and it gave us time to talk. We talked about how we feel like we'll be alone forever. How do we even find a man to want us with two kids in the picture? Especially when we're so hypocritical and don't want someone with kids (*messy x 2*). It felt so hopeless.

For weeks, I'd been meaning to sign up for some daily emails that DivorceCare sends out. I found them so helpful in getting through that first year. While on the site, I looked up locations near Jeff to see if there was anywhere he could attend. There wasn't, and in my area—only two groups. I mean, what were the odds?! How did I come to join this church that was just right for me? I never would have found this group otherwise, and I wouldn't have known I needed it. I'm amazed at how much it helped heal me. And it was just another smack in my face of God trying to steer my life to a better place and help me find Him.

Sometimes, I think about being a single mom and wonder if it made me a worse mom overall. I was tired, easily frustrated, yelled more often—I didn't feel like I was as present as I should be. Because I just couldn't give them one hundred percent of me. I wanted to. Really. I am just not wired to. And the saddest part is that bedtime wasn't fun for me anymore. It used to be one of my favorites—not because I was about to have "me" time once they were out, but because it was snuggly and loving and sweet. Don't get me wrong—it was still all those things, but now it was combined with stress—and TWO kids. I didn't get to enjoy time with one because I was thinking about the other. And for so long, it was such a battle with Peyton that there was nothing fun at all. At least Ryan still let me sing him to sleep and snuggle and hug.

All that said, I know I was an incredible mom during this time. Super Mom. Even though we don't have a perfect life, we never did before. And now, even though we were a family of three, we were a *happy* family of three. There was no random yelling; no outbursts. Things were peaceful. Easy. Loving. It was so much better without Jeff's toxic behavior in our home.

The decrease in disposable income was one of the hardest practical changes I went through during the divorce. I've always been so good with money, such a good saver, maintaining a high emergency fund, and every time I had to penny pinch or watch my savings dwindle, it was a punch in the gut. The lawyer fees killed me. After the initial five-thousand dollars in the spring, I paid her another twenty-three hundred and literally Nothing. Had. Happened. I was terrified of these escalating costs and unsure what to do. I wanted everything done so badly, but I didn't want to give him what he didn't deserve—and what he'd throw away on booze and other nonsense.

Then finally, the day before Thanksgiving, Jeff and I officially settled. Jeff signed after some final, stressful arguments about how much he owed in back child support. I totally blew up at my lawyer and dreaded my bill from her. The agreement wasn't perfect, but it could have been worse. Here's the hard truth if you've never been there—I gave him $25,000 in assets + paid $10k in lawyer fees. It felt like the end of the world and made things really tight, but the reality is so many end up in places far worse. I have a friend who is in six figures with the amount she's lost thanks to her divorce battle. I never had to tap into my retirement funds, and I know most of my friends did. Divorce battles drain so many of their future funds.

So now that he'd signed, the protective order was dissolved. I had no idea how he'd behave once he's allowed to talk to me. Would he text a million apologies? Call me? Email me? Not apologize at all? Did he think I still loved him? That we had a chance?

Even though I knew a million percent that I would go through with the divorce, I still wanted to see that Jeff loved me, and I was waiting for that apology. I was honestly stupid enough to expect him to show up at the door with flowers. That never happened. He was still totally in love with me, but he was too prideful to admit any fault and just expected me to melt back into his arms. Honestly. That's what he thought would happen.

At some point after the beach trip with his family, Chris finally got fed up being in the middle and stopped engaging as the mediator between everyone—me, his parents, Jeff.

I let him know about the settlement, and when I told him via text that the "next step" was just to wait until June when I could file for divorce, I got this response:

You've made up your mind on this? You don't even want to see what it'll be once you get to talk to one another? Not talking so long made it such a strain on both of you and there were so many misunderstandings... He had no money and apparently my family thinks they're helping him get back on his feet. I don't agree with everything they've done but a lot of it he didn't ask for. I don't know, just don't want to see a family get divorced unless it's 100% necessary.

I mean, I know it's easy to misinterpret meaning in a text, but that was pretty direct. I was livid. I fully expect that opinion from people who don't know my whole story, because I didn't believe in divorce either. But now I do—when the circumstances demand it. It was just the most painful comment from someone I never expected. I was really sad for how little our lives may cross in the future. How could I go and stay with them without Jeff? How could I act like I'm a part of their family when it's so clear that I'm not?

But the reality is, feelings change. The further you separate from these painful moments, the less painful they become. Even the memories of them start to fade. If I didn't have all of mine written out, I never would have remembered that text from Chris. We say and feel a lot when we're in the thick of our troubles, and those will pass.

While the kids and I don't get to see Chris and Beth and their kids more than once a year, we *do* still see them. They're still very much a part of our lives, and I'm grateful for everything they've done to make that happen for all of us.

Chapter 11

Disappointment and letdown

Peyton started taking a Saturday morning gymnastics class. I texted Jeff on a Friday to see if he wanted to join us or come over after.

"Come over after," he replied.

I texted him the next morning and asked him to pick up bananas for Ryan, his current favorite food.

"No problem," he texted back.

At ten-thirty, when he was supposed to be here, I get a text that he had to reschedule. He had "a deer under the car."

The message wasn't, "I hit a deer."

It was, "I have a deer underneath my car. I don't know if it did any damage underneath the car."

Okay, great, so check your car. Or switch cars. Or come in a few hours. Seriously? You "need to reschedule" and that's it?

I hated that we were outside playing and waiting for him to come when I got the text. So then comes Mommy having to break the bad news of her dad yet again.

"I don't think Daddy's coming today."

"Whyyyyy?" Peyton said, and came over to me with tears.

The good thing about a four-year-old though, is that she can forget about things pretty quickly. I asked her if she wanted to go shopping and get a car wash (Don't ask. She loves the foam!), and she was happy as a clam. She asked about him once or twice more, but then she was fine.

It had been over two weeks since he'd last seen the kids—on the day after Thanksgiving for about forty-five minutes. How can he stand it?

I had no idea if he ever told the truth about the deer. I checked his phone records, and he didn't call anyone. Not his parents, not an insurance company, not a tow truck. All normal things to do if you really did hit a deer. So, I used my poor daughter as a pawn (guilty 🙍) and had her call his parents. Jeff's mom answered and Peyton asked for her dad. His mom had no idea he never showed, no clue about the deer, and said she'd call him and check.

Jeff didn't call his mom back for over an hour. Sounds like he was deer *hunting* to me, not hit by a deer. He'd made calls to an old work friend, and I think it was one who shot deer on his property.

Jeff called Peyton back that night as we were on our way out the door to go see Christmas lights. She asked if he was going to see her tomorrow, and he had the nerve to reply, "That's up to your mom."

At least she was too young to understand that manipulation, but I hoped he would learn to co-parent better than that.

I think the part that was hardest for me that day was realizing that I was still *expecting* from him. Expecting him to be kind, to try and win me back, to be responsible, to be helpful. I just didn't know what I saw happening in our future. It was just more reasons to assume he was out there drinking the days away.

Up to that point, he'd never been one to bail on his kids. Why do it today? On his first day when he was going to see me. Did he get nervous and drink? Did he just think it was a great day to go deer hunting? Did a deer really hit his car at 10AM? The not knowing was so hard. Control freaks like me need to know it all.

Since his phrase of "That's up to your mom" was to be taken literally — he didn't ask me to come over or make any hint that he wanted to plan something. I texted him a few hours later and he said he'd come, but I certainly wasn't telling Peyton in advance.

Jeff did end up coming the following day, and he brought the bananas I'd asked for. He had a great visit with the kids, and it just broke my heart that they didn't get to see him more often. He didn't have the ability to care for them, but he was fabulous at playing with them and loving on them.

I continued practicing not having expectations of him, but I couldn't believe he didn't really talk to me. No apology. Or asking if there was hope. Did he care? Because I think he did. But he made me doubt.

He never initiated any conversation with me that day and tried to keep things short when I asked him questions. It was painful. And sad. I just wanted to rush through this part and see us get to a good place.

***

By now it was Christmas, the first one on our own. For some reason, we didn't get many Christmas cards that year. Was this the year people decided they just didn't have the energy for them? Or did people not send one to me because they didn't know how to address it? Didn't want to send it to a broken family? I don't know. I know I'm crazy, but that critical voice in my head made me wonder things like that. All the ways we were outcasts now.

My parents spent the night on Christmas Eve and were here in the morning when the kids got up. Peyton wanted a *Tangled* crown, gloves, and *Tangled* hair and was over the moon with her new gear and loved the giant unicorn stuffed animal that Santa surprised her with. Ryan cried and didn't like his giant hugging Elmo at first, but eventually he warmed up and was giving Elmo hugs.

I sent Jeff pictures that morning and wished him a Merry Christmas. That afternoon he called and wanted to talk. I decided to stop avoiding it and went upstairs from everyone and let him talk.

It really just grazed the surface of all the things he should have said, and it did nothing to satisfy the level of apology I wanted from him. But just the same, it was devastating to hear. He was so sad and so lonely. He still loved me so much and wanted nothing more than to be back here. Even if his words lacked what I wanted to hear.

He called to say he wanted my approval to enlist in the Navy. He said he was meeting with a recruiter next week. While that's all well and good, I would have been shocked if he was able to follow-through with it—either on his own or if the Navy would actually accept him.

He said he wanted to let me know because it would mean that he wouldn't be able to see the kids for a long time. He says he was enlisting to show he was serious about bettering himself for us.

Once again, "for us."

"Jeff, I think that's great. You should do everything you can to make yourself better for your kids, but I don't want you thinking about me as part of that equation."

I didn't have the heart to come out with it on Christmas and say, "No, of course there is no hope for us. I would never let you in this home again."

But by God, I hoped we could have the best, most amicable relationship imaginable. I hoped we could talk and be friends and be great co-parents to our kids.

And maybe we really would be able to do that.

The next few days didn't go so well though.

First, he no showed twice after Christmas.

Then he texted me on New Year's Eve wanting to talk to him about our future so he can know before going into the new year. I let him talk first, still wanting to hear an apology. His apologies always ended with something about how he regrets giving up all he had—his family, his home, and me. But in my head, all I hear is, "I messed up so bad and now look at this shit life I'm leading—making no money, living in my parents' house, and not being with you."

It's the kind of apology you'd EXPECT from someone who lost it all. It's not the sincere one where he takes accountability and says, "Wow, I'm so sorry for all of the pain I caused you, for ruining your dreams and destroying our family. I'm sorry that our kids aren't growing up with two parents, and I'm sorry that I was so irresponsible with my life and unable to be an adult."

Now, if I heard that, I'd believe there was change.

That New Year's Eve conversation ended with me telling him to, "Shut up and listen to me while I talk."

We were getting nowhere, so I hung up. And he called back FIFTEEN times. I never replied and he eventually gave up.

Happy New Year!

He visited the next day and we didn't speak at all. That night, I emailed him:

I have so much to say but just never know what or when to share. So I just wanted to say that I love you terribly, and I have been in agony since your last night in rehab because I knew you were coming home not committed to being sober. That following week and month was the worst of my life. I don't know how I survived the summer taking care of our children. I was constantly exhausted, depressed, and hiding it all from our impressionable and sad little girl. She had such a hard time adjusting to our new life and not understanding it. She acted out at school, slept on my floor every night, and asked where you were. Any thought of you brought me to tears, and I didn't want to talk to anyone. In the fall, I started attending a support group for people who are separated, and it helped tremendously. That 2 hours is the highlight of my week because it gets to be all about me, how I feel, and how I'm supposed to heal. I've made a few friends in the group, so we all get to be depressed together. When Peyton was talking about our "party" we had before Christmas, it was with 4 of those women and their kids.

I don't believe that you've been sober since leaving jail, but I believe you are trying your hardest. All I've ever wanted is honesty from you. And I have no idea if I'll ever get it. I can't be with you because I can't trust you or believe in you. And there's nothing worse in the world. Not having the love of my life and the father of my children will haunt me forever, and I hope you never take another drink and make me regret not being with you. But since I can't trust you'll do that, I have no choice.

A part of me was expecting you to write me, call me, or show up at the house the moment you were allowed to. An apology for the right things. And then nothing. Still nothing. That's my fault because I let you get away with treating me like that for too many years. It's made you think that all you need to do is give me a blanket apology and expect me to accept it. But I don't. I've worked so hard to start healing, and I can go days without crying now. I don't feel like you're even trying to make this a hard decision for me.

Your kids love you and are too young to know all of the mistakes you've made. Don't let them down. You're lucky that for now, they just get the fun parts of you. You aren't responsible for their care, and you mostly get to just play and have fun. I hope that you'll expand your visits with them outside of the house, but you can't expect me to make those plans for you. It's up to you if you utilize your visitations.

I really do hope that you and I get to a place where we can be friends and talk and have a good relationship. Our kids deserve that, and I doubt you want us to deal with each other for the next 17 years if we aren't able to communicate.

You are a good person, and you deserve good things.

Please no more late night phone calls. No calling 15 times. Those kind of things don't scream sober to me.

He replied that night and had somehow turned that email into a message of hope for us and offered to get rid of his Xbox, sell his guns, and never wear camouflage again. Wow, he sure knew the way to my heart, huh? To be fair, he also told me that there weren't words to even apologize for everything and he didn't know where to begin.

The next day he called me "to talk." By that, I assumed he wanted to have another serious talk—an apology, talk of the future, something. Nope. He literally meant "to talk." He asked me how my day was, what I did, what we had for dinner, and what book I was reading. I told him I didn't feel like that kind of conversation was appropriate right now since we weren't together. He didn't like that.

After that, things went downhill. It was a positive for me though because it was crystal clear proof that he hadn't changed at all. Maybe he wasn't drinking, or maybe he was, but the fundamental problems still existed.

He accused me of throwing away our marriage for *one mistake.* "Does 'til death do us part mean nothing to you? I would never cheat on you. I've never even thought of cheating on you," he said.

When I told him that they weren't remotely the same—cheating isn't dangerous, threatening, or aggressive, he was so pissed. He considered cheating much worse—since he didn't do it, I guess!

Great, but instead, he'd screamed in my face, shoved me, punched a hole in our wall, drove drunk with our children. The list goes on. A lot worse than cheating, I think. Not to say I'd forgive cheating either, but the more I look at marriage, the more I think I probably could. A cheater can still be a present parent, a provider, and be kind. An alcoholic cannot.

One night, Jeff wanted to talk to Peyton before bed, and she said she wanted him to come live with her. She wanted to visit him at his home. She said the "build man" could make her a room. And she wanted a princess bed. She asked why he couldn't live with us at our house, and he replied, "You'll have to ask your mom."

Ugh. Why is it so hard for adults to put their kids first and not try to manipulate the situation or place blame on the ex?

When she hung up, I explained that it will be a while before Daddy would be able to get his own house because he needs a lot of money to do that.

She replied, "Well I can empty my piggy-bank and give it to Daddy. Then he can have a house."

Oh, bless her sweet heart. I told her it would take more money than what was in her piggy-bank, and she said she would find more banks and more treasures. And she'd find treasure for me and Ryan too. It was just the sweetest thing I'd ever heard.

Her innocence through all of this turmoil overwhelmed me sometimes. It was hard to remember that she was just four years old and what she'd say isn't necessarily what she meant, or what's right for her. She didn't have the ability to process all of the change around her. And it was my job to find ways to connect with her, and help her process her emotions.

At the end of the book, you'll find a list of children's books that I used and found helpful.

Chapter 12

Single moments

One of the hardest parts of recovery for me was walking around and thinking I'm doing well, and I haven't cried for days or weeks, and then suddenly, something totally insignificant or one errant thought would just get the waterworks flowing.

This time, it was an Ed Sheeran song. I was listening to his beautiful, sweet voice and imagining what it will be like if I met someone one day who swept me off my feet. Someone who totally wow'd me. Someone who made me feel like the most important person in the world. I pictured a wedding—which I fully believed I wouldn't have again—but I thought, "This time, I would have it in my church. I would invite those people who saw me through this crisis and brought me through to the other side."

I pictured myself just crying the whole way through the ceremony because I could imagine how that would feel to find someone willing to love me and give me the world—and fully embrace my kids as his.

Jeff's visits over the next month were uneventful. He always visited at our house in the hopes that he could see me and we could talk. I found my situation very unique compared to the girlfriends I had who were going through this with me. In their cases, it was mutual that they didn't want to be together. In my case, it was all me. That was really hard to face. I continued to question if I was failing in God's eyes and if I should be supporting Jeff through this and be by his side.

But my rational side was there reminding me that if he was here, he'd still be drunk, probably dead. He'd be in our lives everyday making us miserable. By leaving him, he was forced to face his situation. He was so sad and so scared, and that was hard for me to watch. It was hard for me to look at this man I promised to love forever and only see him as a sad and lonely friend.

I went to a friend's baby shower and this woman I've known for years bombarded me with nosy questions. It didn't feel like someone who wanted to see how I was or truly cared; rather, it felt intrusive.

She asked me if my mom was helping me pay for daycare. "Isn't that really expensive? How can you pay for that?"

In the words of Stephanie Tanner, "How Ruuuude!"

I was appalled. It was hard enough being single with two little ones, but I was damn proud of being able to provide for them and not change our lifestyle. Yes, my parents had gifted me things here and there, but I'd have been fine without the help too. They offered their support to help limit my stress.

The next week, I went to a Kindergarten Readiness class at Peyton's daycare, and it was all moms and dads together. Me and one other single mom were the only ones without a dad there. It was the first of many things I'd have to do without a partner, and that was scary. And embarrassing. Embarrassment was still my overwhelming emotion—which was even more embarrassing! Why was I so prideful? I was incredibly proud of myself, and those around me were too. But I couldn't focus on that. Because to the outside world (whose opinions should not matter!), I just look like another statistic—giving up on marriage because it was too hard.

———————◆———————

The next step we had in our divorce process was refinancing the house so I could stay in it as the sole owner. In the settlement, I gave Jeff $10,000 as his equity stake in the home. There were so many nuances and dependencies to deal with to make the closing happen, and I hated having to rely on him. If he forgot to show, decided not to, or didn't bring his ID or something—the closing wouldn't happen. And it would screw me over with my interest rate, closing documents, and all that fun stuff.

He did come through for me though. I had to remind him countless times to show up for the closing, and thankfully he did. We had uncomfortable small talk while we waited to sign the paperwork, and he was being totally snarky when he said, "You look happy." {*insert eye roll here*}

Like, what do I say to that? "Yes, I'm happy you showed up. Yes, I'm happy this is the last thing I need you to do. Yes, I'm finally healing and feeling happy." I don't know what he was looking for, other than a reaction.

After we closed, he was scheduled to go visit the kids at daycare and go to their Valentine's Day party. He asked if I wanted to join him.

"This is your time with them," I said. "And I have to go to the grocery store while I have the free time."

I could tell he was upset by that, but instead of expressing that he was hurt, he expressed it as anger. I would later find out that this was a defining moment for him.

By asking me to go with him, he was really asking me *to be with him*, to give him another chance. And when I didn't take the bait, he dove headfirst into a secret relationship that we'd all find out about months later. (I mean, with my sleuthing, I knew about it pretty quick, but he didn't know that.)

Chapter 13

You're dead to me

About a month had passed since we refinanced the house and Jeff had given me his big boombox over-the-head moment by asking me to come with him to the kids' Valentine's party.

And then—I received my first ever DICK PIC. Accidentally. From Jeff. He said that he meant to send it to some guy at work who had sent him one "to **** with him."

All I thought was, "Wow, guys do that? How weird."

I asked a few guy friends if sending dick pics to each other is in fact "something you do" as part of the male species. Turns out, it is not.

Fast forward a few days later, and curiosity got the best of me. I hadn't logged in to look at Jeff's phone records in a long time, and what I found was crazy. The texting was OUT OF CONTROL. Hundreds of texts a day to this one number. And prior to him sending me that picture, he'd received about ten picture texts from the same number.

Clearly this had to be a girl, right? So, I did a reverse phone look up, and sure enough, I was right. The weird part is that I wasn't sad or jealous. I was more irritated that he'd clearly found someone totally trashy. Here they were exchanging naked texts, and I don't even know if they'd been on a date. Where did they meet? At a bar? At AA? Was he drinking with her? Did he spend the night with her? Would he sign the divorce papers now? Would he get her pregnant and give my kids some awful half sibling? That was the question that sickened my stomach most.

He posted on Facebook at 1AM: "Come on Saturday!!!!! New chapter in life. New beginning."

At first, I thought maybe he found a better job or was moving out, but neither of those really made sense. And when Chris and Beth both posted asking what the new chapter was, he didn't respond. So, I was able to deduce—it was a date with this chick.

The saddest part of his "new chapter" was that he bailed on a visit with his kids in order to have this Saturday with her. He told me he had a doctor's appointment (on a Saturday…) *and* needed to take his car in because it was acting up. Typical Jeff lies that just rolled off the tongue.

When Jeff was in rehab, there were classes for family members to attend during the weekend visits. One thing I learned about Jeff, and alcoholics in general, is that they tend to get stuck at the age where they first start drinking. So, Jeff was an adolescent. The way he'd behave and react in situations—it was that of a 15-year-old. When someone pissed him off, he'd cut them out of his life. I was shocked I lasted as long as I did before he cut me out too.

In addition to this new girl in his life, Jeff started giving other signs that his drinking had returned full force. Jeff played a lot of video games with his brother, which was always a good bonding time for them. But it was also how Chris knew when Jeff was drinking. So, when Jeff came to the house for his next visit, I decided it was time to start breathalyzing him—something that was a part of our custody agreement. I could breathalyze him any time he was going to be with the kids.

When he came in with lunch, I asked him to take the test, and he just looked up at me with a little smirk and said, "Nope. I read the agreement last night, and I only have to do it if I'm driving them. You can no longer control me. You're dead to me."

I panicked that we didn't execute the agreement properly, so I emailed my lawyer to ask. Thankfully she said his driving is immaterial, and he had to submit to a test. But even if he didn't—wasn't his behavior and attitude all I needed for confirmation? Why would he bother trying to find a loophole to allow him to drink around the kids if he wasn't actually drinking?

As he was leaving, I said, "I'm sorry I am dead to you, but I don't feel that way about you."

I brought up the dick pic and accused him of sleeping with someone—which he denied—but he didn't say there was *no* girl.

A week went by and he hadn't asked to see the kids. Didn't call. Nothing. And I couldn't have ever imagined it, but that was the last time I'd ever see him and one of the final times we'd ever talk.

Easter was a few weeks later, and Jeff was supposed to come and spend the afternoon with the kids and then make dinner. He texted me at 11:36AM, while we were outside having an Egg Hunt with my neighbors, that he was up sick all night and wasn't coming. I had two thoughts on this:

He knew he'd fail a breathalyzer if he came.

Maybe he really did try to not drink leading up to his visit today, but he was back to drinking so much again that it made him go into withdrawal.

Later that week he texted me, "I've been cleared by the doctor and do not have Shingles, so I want to see the kids at school next week."

It'd be just like Jeff to make up a story like that. And then here I go second guessing myself and wondering if it was true. He did get a bad rash the previous summer, so WAS he telling the truth? This is the nonsense that was going to drive me to a crazy house. I could never know what is true, and I'd always jump to terrible conclusions, which were probably the right ones. Based on his texting and phone behavior on Easter, it looks like he'd spent the day with his new sexting buddy.

He did end up coming to the daycare that next week to have lunch with the kids. It had been a month since his last visit went down at my house, and when he met them at daycare, he spent thirty minutes with Ryan and fifteen minutes with Peyton. Fifteen minutes. That's all he could dedicate to her. Our daycare bent over backwards to make it easy for him too. They were always allowed to go hang out in a conference room for as long as they wanted.

He had totally faded. He stopped calling them or asking to call. He was off the following weekend and was going to pick up his remaining things from the house. I had them all packed for him to come pick up, and I asked if he wanted to spend time with the kids, and he said no. He literally drove an hour to our house and chose NOT to visit with them.

We were in the backyard playing when I heard him pull up in *her* car, and he didn't even pop his head around to say hello. It was like living in a movie. Totally unreal. I couldn't help myself and had to run inside to peek out the window. I couldn't get my eyes on her, but I managed to get a glimpse of a heinous tattoo on Jeff's calf though. That was new. An animal of some sort, I think. It was gross. And a sure sign he was spiraling out of control.

Instead of saying hello, on the front porch was a *Frozen* music box and two toy cars. Seriously. THAT was his substitute.

In that moment, I was disappointed in my choice for a spouse. How was it possible for someone to let me down so incredibly much? God was taking care of me in SO MANY WAYS to compensate for him, but it was still so painful. It was like he was slowly falling out of love with the kids. I knew he would be out of their lives in another year. As long as he kept this path and kept drinking, that's what was going to happen. I was devastated for them. It had been almost a year to the day that he'd left for rehab. I wondered where he'd be in another twelve months.

Chapter 14

What is a family?

I couldn't believe it, but Peyton would start Kindergarten in the fall. I don't know what other counties are like, but in ours, everyone goes on the same day in the Spring prior to starting in order to register kids. You have to bring documents proving your residency and the kids have to take a placement test that checks their knowledge of things like counting, identifying shapes, and knowing their phone number.

While I was so excited for her to have this moment and know that smaller daycare bills were just a few months away, the registration process was humiliating for someone going through a divorce. I had to bring our custody papers and they put a big "C" with a circle on Peyton's file. She was one of "those" kids. I wanted to crawl under a rock. No ring on my finger and this sweet little firecracker who the teacher called a "very smart little girl."

There's a lot that I never would have thought of prior to this experience. Daddy-daughter dances, Donuts with Dad, Muffins with Mom. At daycare, the kids were supposed to bring a "Family picture" to share, and I didn't even send one because I didn't know what to bring. One of the *two* family photos we had of the four of us? Did I send one in of just the three of us? One of the three of us, and one of them with Jeff?

There is so much out there celebrating the traditional nuclear family, which I think is wonderful and an ideal situation, but since it wasn't *my* situation, events that celebrate families just remind me of ours being different. And it was teaching the kids that they were different. Not that these aren't great life lessons to have, and I know in the end, it will make them more resilient, more compassionate, and more open-minded. But it's still added to my plate of things I had to explain.

Weeks had gone by and we still didn't hear from Jeff. Out of the blue, on the way home from daycare, Peyton said, "I miss my daddy. I never see him anymore. I'll never see him again."

I told her we could call him when we got home. But by then she'd forgotten, so I didn't bring it up again. What would make my sweet baby girl say she'll never see her daddy again? How does she know?

The next day, she asked about him again. She just cried, "Where IS he?"

126

I tried to explain that, like her cousins, he doesn't live near us, so it was hard to see him a lot. I doubt he'd even pick up the phone if I called, but I really struggled if that was the right move. In my heart, the right thing was to let her talk to her dad whenever she wants to. But also, I didn't want him constantly breaking her heart, and the less involved he was, the less she'll think about him.

But then I'd question myself. Was that really true? I felt endless pain trying to decide what was best for everyone. It was so much pressure trying to decide for these little munchkins the right way to handle a single parent life when their dad may end up being a deadbeat, someone in and out of their lives for years.

I finally couldn't contain my curiosity anymore, and I called my sister-in-law. She called out that I'd changed my name on Facebook, and I told her that Jeff bringing his girlfriend to my house was the final straw, and it was the perfect segue to talk to her about everything that had been going down. Chris actually got on the phone too, and it was the first time in five months that we'd spoken.

Chris said that about six weeks earlier, he and Jeff were playing video games and he could tell Jeff was drinking—playing sloppy and disappearing for a long time. The next day, Chris texted him and said that he was disappointed in him and didn't want to play if Jeff was going to be drinking. Jeff just texted back that **he** was disappointed in Chris for thinking he was drinking again. And they hadn't spoken since.

Chris said that Jeff didn't ever speak to his parents, despite still living in their basement. They had no clue what he did in his room all day long. He was always down there with the door closed.

It really speaks to a parent's love and difficulty to end enablement when they could tolerate living with that kind of behavior. They wouldn't travel or leave him alone because they didn't trust him to be alone, and yet, they'd prefer this stressful situation to be happening under their roof than to leave him to his own defensives. This was the same sense of enablement I struggled with before I realized that cutting things cold turkey was going to give him his best chance to grow through this.

I was surprised to hear that no one knew anything about his girlfriend, but Chris called her "the perfect companion for his spiraling behavior." She was either in the same condition as him, or she was clueless, and he was hiding it all from her. We all felt like we were losing any connection to him.

I think a lot about how tragic it is to lose a loved one and grieve for that person. I remember thinking about it non-stop after Jeff moved out—when I was grieving for him and for the family we no longer were. It's a pain that's so real and so crushing that even once you're clean and through the other side, it can still strike and make you relive the loss and pain all over again.

After not hearing from him for weeks, and having Peyton's sad words echo in my ears all week, I texted Jeff and said, "Do you have plans to ever see the kids again?"

He replied later that night with, "I have been working the whole last two weeks. Just getting out of work now. Sorry it is so late."

That's it. Not, "Hey, I'm off Tuesday and would love to go to school and see them." Or, "I miss them and have been meaning to call to talk to them." Nothing.

I so badly wanted a crystal ball to see how our lives would play out, to know if he was in or out. Was he constantly going to let them down? Or would he make a decision one way or the other to be present or not? And what decision did I want him to make? I really didn't know, but I think I wanted him in. My heart wanted that, but my head wasn't so sure. I doubted him and the impact he would have on them. How did I keep this from destroying them?

Peyton mentioned her piggy-bank for the first time in forever and said she wanted to give her money to her daddy for a house so she could "spend four days with him." She asked me if I could give him money for a house. She asked why she never sees him. Why he never sees her.

I truly didn't know what to tell her. Every part of me wanted her to know the truth, but it was not time for that. When would it be time? Five years? Seven? When he completely falls off the radar?

Unsurprisingly, Jeff had gone radio silent. I had no idea if he was going to come to Peyton's upcoming preschool graduation and see her. I had no idea if he was going to see the kids ever again. I don't know what was going on in his head, but it was scary. It was simply *beyond words* HEARTBREAKING that this man I trusted with my whole world had abandoned us so completely, had become entirely consumed by alcohol that he gave up everything in his world.

It was humiliating for me, but it was devastating for my kids. Sometimes, I'd make the mistake of getting on Google and looking up things like "absent dad" and there was nothing harder for me than seeing the odds stacked against my kids. How was I supposed to deal with that? How was it supposed to make me feel?

Trust me, I know I'm one of the lucky ones—able to support us and not uproot our lives. I had the means to take care of them (although seeing my bank account fall to $432 was an eye opener). I had a dad and brother who were so good to Peyton and Ryan. God willing, they would be around to be role models and give them constant male figures. I had support all around.

The preschool graduation was doing superlatives. I had a little girl who thought she was getting the "happy award" or the "smiley award." Now what did that tell me? Yes, her daddy was breaking her heart, but she was resilient, and I was doing a damn good job.

In the midst of the sad and depressing articles I was reading about absent dads, this quote struck me, reminding me that all hope wasn't lost, and I could manage this:

*Statistics claim that parenting alone can put your child at high risk for drug use, early sexuality, assaults, depression and suicide attempts. I could go on and on, but **the ultimate thing I want moms to know is that these are just statistics. This is not your family.... This is not you!***

You are in charge of your destiny. You have the power to make your family consist of well-educated, self-confident and happy people. Don't allow HIM the power to do your family more wrong. (PaulaHenry1 2011)

I knew this. I did. But it was hard to remember all the time. And in the end, I felt like her life couldn't be as good as it would be with a good dad. And Ryan, he couldn't even express to me in words how not having a dad affected him. He'd show me—when he would sob and break down when Jeff would leave, when he'd see any picture and say "Dada, dada" over and over, and when he would look like the happiest boy on the planet when his dad would visit. I wasn't a fool to think he wasn't getting screwed up too. But I hoped he was getting all the love and affection that he needs from me at this point.

I pictured a day in another year or two when he'd start to want his daddy more and realize the absence in his life. And I'd have to start all over trying to explain. And what would Peyton understand at that point? And what *would* Jeff's interaction be by then? Attempting sobriety and parenting? A drunk? Married again? A father to a new bastard child? Oh dear Lord, there are few things I prayed for more than for Jeff **not** to bring another innocent baby into this world. That baby doesn't deserve it. Whatever mother he were to find would not be equipped to handle a baby on her own. *That* baby would be one of the statistics.

Chapter 15

Letting God lead

I used to hate that the courts require you to wait a year to get divorced, but now, I think it's so smart. I got to be mostly private at work and on social media while I was crying multiple times a day at the thought of my life's drama. When I finally changed my name at work, I got lots of "Congrats" emails from people who assumed I got married. And it didn't really bother me or embarrass me. I simply told them it was "reverse congratulations." And when my co-worker successfully called me "Ashley Adams" in a meeting, I congratulated her on not stumbling. But it hit me when she did that, that I really wasn't bothered. I would have been in tears nine months or six months ago if I had to acknowledge my separation in any way to someone. That one year waiting period, if used correctly, can truly be a time of healing.

I'm not even sure when I acknowledged that I *was* healing. My theme song that whole first year was "Stronger" by Sara Evans. I'd literally turn it on in the car just so I could cry all the way to work and get it out of my system. It was a good thing I have long eyelashes and could get away without mascara. No waterproof brand would have been strong enough. But there's a line in that song about waking up and realizing that you haven't cried in weeks. And that's kind of how it went. The daily crying to and from work slowed to just 'to' work. Then a few times a week. Then listening to the song one day I thought, "Wait, when *was* the last time I cried?"

I was getting better.

One area where I continued to struggle, was explaining *why* I got divorced. I wanted to so badly. I wanted people to feel for me and say, "Wow, you're so strong." I didn't want them judging me for just giving up on my marriage without knowing why.

But when I took a step back, I would have absolutely felt someone was oversharing with me if I worked with someone and they told me why they got divorced. It was so hard, but I had to allow people to judge me.

Around this time, I'd been listening to a bible study in the car— something that eighteen months ago, I couldn't have dreamed of doing, and look at me now. God had become such a focal point for me, and I continue to be amazed at the miracles and blessings that kept finding their way to me.

In this particular bible study, the speaker talked about how it often takes rejection for people to find Jesus. I never would have put it in those words on my own, but it was true for me. I never would have gotten so into finding and learning about God without this experience in my life.

Is this how He wanted me to submit to Him? To prove my faith in Him? Because it worked. I was there. I **missed** church when I had to go a whole week without being there. I relished my Wednesday bible study group. I learned so much and felt so much more in tune with myself and my emotions.

I had many reasons that church entered my life at this particular time. I knew I was about to need a support system, and what better place to find that than church? The Wednesday night bible study introduced me to an entire network of women of all ages and life experiences. And just as important, going to church gave me an hour to myself. No kids. No family. Just me. Sometimes that felt really lonely in worship on Sundays when I'd see couples and families, but most of the time, I just liked being with myself. It was peaceful and emotional. I don't know what it is, but as soon as music would start playing, I'd lose it. Tears would flow, and I'd think about how awful everything was. I think losing it then is what helped me keep it together most of the time during the rest of the week.

Plus, Peyton and Ryan loved our church. They got to play and be with other kids. Ryan, being the angel he is, was adored by the nursery volunteers. And Peyton's favorite thing about her Sunday School room was getting two dixie cups of marshmallows as a snack each week—which was more sugar than I allowed, but what was I gonna do? I'd tell her she could have one, and she'd say, "Okay Mommy. But don't tell the teacher that."

---◆---

Whenever Peyton would get in trouble or cry, she'd decide to talk about Jeff. One night, through tears she said, "Mommy, why doesn't Daddy want to see me?"

Why doesn't he WANT to see me? How could she even say that? Know that? My heart sank. At first, she caught me off guard and I said, "I don't know."

But then I regained my composure, and I told her it was just because he didn't live nearby. And just like she didn't get to see her cousins a lot, she couldn't see her daddy a lot—something she'd heard before and had been my go-to response.

What else could I do to reassure her? How else could I make sure she felt like she was getting everything she needed? Clearly not having a dad hurt her. I never thought someone could let me down like this. I never thought that I'd marry a man BECAUSE I THOUGHT HE'D MAKE A GREAT DAD and he would turn out to be a deadbeat. The irony is not lost on me.

Sheryl Sandberg, COO of Facebook and author of *Lean In* was one of my soul sisters during this period of my life. First, her book *Lean In* reminded me just how powerful I was and really inspired me to keep my focus at work and not let a bad boss or a bad situation set me back.

But then, just as I was dealing with all of this insanity in my own life, Sheryl lost her husband—her wonderful and kind husband who left behind two young girls in her capable, but insanely busy, hands. She wrote the most beautiful message about him on Facebook that would become the theme of her future book, *Option B*. In her case, it relates to death, but perfectly explained the pain of any loss, and it spoke so deeply to what I was experiencing at the time and continued to go through as a single parent.

Here's the excerpt from my favorite section of her post:

I was talking to [a friend] about a father-child activity that Dave is not here to do. We came up with a plan to fill in for Dave. I cried to him, "But I want Dave. I want option A." He put his arm around me and said, "Option A is not available. So let's just kick the shit out of option B."

Dave, to honor your memory and raise your children as they deserve to be raised, I promise to do all I can to kick the shit out of option B. And even though sheloshim has ended, I still mourn for option A. I will always mourn for option A. (Sandberg, June 2015)

Let's kick the shit out of option B! Could there be a better mantra for life? Kind of like, when Plan A doesn't work, don't worry—there are twenty-five more letters in the alphabet.

I kept looking for guidance on how to handle Jeff and Peyton. She talked about him on a daily basis. One night she did her prayers and she told God she was never going to see her daddy again.

She was doing it all the time now. My sweet little girl. We were looking at her calendar and she pointed out Father's Day. She asked if she would see her daddy that day. I said I didn't know, but we could spend the day with Pop Pop, my dad. She didn't like Option B. How can I teach her about kicking the shit out of Option B?

My other soul sister, always, is the one and only Taylor Swift. She always knows just how to get at my soul.

There's something about her words that resonate with so many situations. Something about every album that finds a way to pierce my heart and simultaneously shatter it and complete it.

To date, I've found that her song *Clean* is the one that just *gets* me. At her *1989* concert I went to that summer, she introduced the song with this:

You are someone who is wiser because you've gone through terrible things and you continue to get out of bed and get on with things. You are someone who maybe even has a lot on your mind right now, but you are at a concert having the BEST TIME EVER. And I think that a lot of us if we've walked through a bunch of rainstorms and we've been through a bunch of things, we feel like we might have scars from that, we feel insecure about that, feel like we might be damaged goods or something. But one thing I've learned in 25 years—and I'm still learning every day—pain and going through pain is awful at the time but it does actually make you stronger. And having insecurities is terrible but it does drive you to do more and accomplish more... (Raleigh, NC 1989 tour)

I've always been a person who has survived through music. While some people may have spent money on partying or shopping when they were younger, I always spent money on CDs and concerts. I love music. Feel good music. Pop music. And now, country music. The songs just make me *feel*. Most of the time I want to feel happy and carefree, but sometimes I want to have a good cry.

Eventually, I thought, the tears had to all come out and leave me *Clean*. I love Taylor's *1989* album (as I do ALL of her albums), but there's always a song or two where I can just Have. A. Moment. And *Clean* is that song for this album. I think that's what I've always loved about music. You can find yourself in them and feel like you aren't alone in having hard times—or good times.

I'd been looking forward to surprising Peyton to see Taylor for literally eight months and two days since I bought the tickets to that summer concert in Raleigh, NC. I had it built up in my mind for far too long. Don't get me wrong—she was so excited and had a blast, but she was only four and a half and was also clingy, tired and not nearly as loud and excited as I thought she'd be.

I had to hold her the entire show, and after every song, she asked if it was over. Not because she wanted it to be but because she had no idea what a concert really was and didn't know she'd hear so many songs! Then after about an hour, she'd had enough. For a girl who never really complains about being tired or actually wants to sleep, she kept crying to me, "Mommy, I'm SO tired!"

I got her to fall asleep in her chair eventually, and she slept for the last three songs. But "Shake it Off" is her favorite, and the "hey hey hey" interlude is HER PART. And even though I woke her up, she was groggy and had her head on my shoulder. I still remind her all these years later about missing her favorite song.

———————◆———————

Ever since I had flat out asked Jeff if he was going to be completely out of his kids' lives, it had been radio silence. Is that not the saddest thing ever? I was praying a lot for guidance on how much to push him on visiting with them. I didn't feel like I had a sense yet of what to do. And I think the answer was that as long as I didn't feel good about it, I keep on trying.

In *The Best Yes*, Lysa Terkeurst writes about reaching out to a friend who was going to give her the RIGHT advice, not just the advice she wanted to hear. And I really had to push myself to live this when I found out that Jeff had lied to me about why he couldn't pick up the furniture from my house that we'd decided he should have.

All I knew was that he was at the beach with his new girlfriend. Our beach. Like, within one hundred yards of the house we'd been renting for the last five years. So close to where we stay that he was visiting the same seafood store and sitting out by the same pier.

I stewed on how to react for over an hour before I decided to let him know that I knew he was at the beach.

"My friend [who owns the house we rent] saw you at the beach. You aren't at work," which was the story he'd told me.

Then I told him I needed him to pick everything up by his original deadline or I was tossing it all.

Then, I paused. I needed validation that was the *right* thing to do.

My friend Courtney told me she'd pick it all up and take it to the dump for me, but I told her no.

I texted Chris and asked if he thought it was forcing consequences on Jeff or if it was mean and vengeful.

The final answer was neither. But it was Beth who was calm and thoughtful enough to talk me through it all. Jeff was sick. He wouldn't look at it as a consequence. It would just be another way I'm screwing him over and how this was all my fault.

She was totally right, of course, but I still struggled that we were feeding into him and working with HIS schedule while he continued to give no consideration to mine or my family's.

At the time, I didn't have a lot of anger towards Jeff. I reserved it for his parents, mostly. Beth reminded me that they were sick too. There was so much enablement and codependence. I knew this, but it didn't help me feel any better.

About six months earlier, his mom had the nerve to complain to Beth about "all the child support" Jeff was giving me and how unfair it was because I was getting everything. Beth, at least, defended me and didn't just sit back and listen to her go on and on. At least, I knew where Jeff was getting it when he would complain about all the child support.

He used to say all the time how I have everything, he has nothing. And while, YES, I did get "everything," that hardly made me a winner in this.

This was *The Hunger Games*—there were no winners. Even the ones who made it out alive had so many scars that it makes it hard to live a normal life again. I knew I would make it out, but not without wounds.

Ryan turned two just before Father's Day, and on his birthday, it was "Desserts with Dad" at daycare. Peyton told me not to go to her classroom because "Mothers aren't allowed." But I told her Pop Pop would come, and I would go to Ryan's room.

When I got there, my dad was already there and had brought Ryan to Peyton's classroom. So, I had ice cream with all of them, and thankfully she welcomed me. I didn't feel weird or embarrassed being the only mom there, and I was glad the kids had me. Parents were all focused on themselves, and who knows if they even thought to assume anything of my presence—they were all men, after all!

That night Jeff actually *called* me on the phone—surely to wish his son a happy birthday, I thought. But no. He wanted to tell me that his dad was coming to get his stuff in the morning, not him, since he had to work.

"And I need to talk to my lawyer because you still owe me money from the 401K"—not that he could comprehend or listen when I told him that it was on him to get the money out. He said he would sign whatever he needed to because he wanted this done now. He also slid in that he wasn't living with his parents anymore, so there was my confirmation that he was with her.

I asked him if he was ever going to see the kids again, and he said, "Yes, but it's gonna be on my terms."

I tried not to let him get to me, but I still found myself shaking with frustration, sadness, and finality when we hung up. I had no idea when I'd talk to him again.

———————◆———————

We were over a year passed our separation, and I was really starting to feel healed on a personal level. I was able to handle the consequences of divorce, speak about it (mostly) without crying, and the kids and I were in a good routine. But I constantly worried about long term, about the unknown. How to function if Jeff stayed an active alcoholic and went in and out of their lives for the next fifteen years. So, I made an appointment to go speak with a child psychologist about the kids, specifically Peyton, so I could have some idea of what I may be up against in the future. How would I talk to her about her dad's absence?

The discussion couldn't have been more depressing. Bottom line, a girl needs to know her dad loves her. No substitute is enough.

The therapist used the words "hugely devastating" in reference to not having both parents in her life. And as painful as those words may feel to me, I needed to push him to be involved and make it all about the kids. Because of his alcoholism, his filter was so distorted and everything I did, whether I had malice behind it or not, felt like I was controlling him.

As for what I could do on my own, and what you can do if you're facing a similar situation—remind them that their daddy loves them. They need a sign that he cares about them. They need to know he's thinking about them. Kindergarten and first grade would be especially hard for them because "Me and my Family" is part of their curriculum. Father's Day is hard enough to contend with, and now I'd get to deal with this from September through June too.

One of the great pieces of advice I got, was to talk to the kids about Jeff as if he had some illness like a brain tumor or something where he couldn't engage with them. Telling them things like, "Your daddy loved watching hockey... he loved watching you ride your bike... When you were born, he..."

Because my memory regularly fails me, I took this advice and used it to actually write the kids each a letter using this concept. Even though the memories and milestones he was here for were few, I could tell it in an impactful way that could hopefully ease their hearts when they're older.

At the end of the day, kids need two things—to know they are loved, and to know they are taken care of. I can provide both of those things. That is within my control. My kids will always know they are loved, even if their dad isn't going to assure them. I will. My parents will. My neighbors and friends will.

When kids are less than six, they don't understand the permanence of things, so it's hard for them to understand that mom and dad won't be together again. I think telling Peyton off the bat that mommies and daddies don't always live together may have actually done some good. And at that age, I did lie to her for the reason she didn't see her dad often. I focused a lot on Jeff's work and that he was in another town, and because of that, he couldn't make frequent visits. Those were the reasons he couldn't see her— not that he didn't love her. For us, it worked. I knew it couldn't be a long-term plan, but in my eyes, it was age appropriate. And if there's anything I've learned with kids, it's that everything is a phase and you always have to come up with new plans as they change and grow.

When she would say her prayers at night, she'd always say that she wants to see her daddy, but I learned to reframe that, too.

"God's taking care of Daddy."

She could pray that God would look after him.

The child therapist left me with some dating advice before our session was over too. At the time, I couldn't imagine a man in our lives, but I was only thirty-two, and I hoped we had a chance to one day.

Keep in mind, these are ideal circumstances. If someone doesn't meet this, it doesn't mean he's not a good person or not good for you. At all. Some of my dearest friends don't meet these rules (I don't meet all these rules!), and we're all still wonderful people that would make great partners. That said, in an ideal scenario, the therapist suggested that I:

1. **Find someone without kids.** The reason for this is just simplicity. Step-parenting is complicated. Adding a new set of children even more so. They may become the best of friends, but they may also act out, get jealous, or feel even more different from their peers than they already did having just you as their mom.

2. **Find someone who has witnessed a good marriage.** Find a man whose parents had a great marriage. Or his best friend had great parents. Some set of adults who showed him how to love a woman. What it means to be a good partner and good parent. It doesn't mean that if his parents are divorced that you're doomed, and he'd be a terrible partner. Just make sure he knows and is willing to do what it takes to make a marriage great.

3. **Not involve him with the kids until it's something stable.** This is such a hard call to make. You want them to meet early so you can gauge the vibe and know if you should keep it going, but you don't want to jump the gun. You don't want to scare the guy off or get him too attached (either out of love or guilt), and you definitely don't want your kids to get too attached to a man and

risk breaking them all over again. That right there is what weighed on my heart every single day when I finally started dating. How far was I willing to go and risk their hearts again?

When I was finally ready to start dating, one of my prescreen questions on eHarmony was "What kind of marriage did/do your parents have?" and the choices basically ranged from loving and respectful to hating each other. It didn't automatically make me rule a guy out, but I was more likely to give someone a chance if they answered in an ideal way for all of my early questions.

Chapter 16

How does The Bachelorette do it?

Other than immediately zooming in on every man's hand to see if there was a ring or not, I'd really stayed away from any thought of dating up to this point. I was and am a huge believer in not dating while going through a separation and honestly, not dating until you're back into a good headspace. Something was wrong in every relationship that ends, and even if you're thinking it wasn't your fault, you still contributed to it in some way.

There is something to be learned—about yourself, about how you handle conflict and relationships, and the men you are attracted to and those who are attracted to you. It's just not realistic that you can learn if you're busy with a new person. And that's not to say that no relationship that starts that way won't work out, but when I saw the divorce rates of second marriages at almost seventy percent, I personally wanted to make sure I did everything in my power to give myself the best chance of success. (Wevorce, 2017)

My divorce papers were filed in June, and I was feeling all the fluttering of a crush with my daughter's swim coach that summer. I didn't know anything about the guy, but he was a teacher and spent his summers coaching swimming, which I grew up doing. And Peyton adored him. I put all these fantasies in my head of what it would be like if we started dating and he became their stepdad. I didn't even know if this guy was single, engaged, or gay. Pretty sure he wasn't gay, but the rest was anyone's guess. I spent the entire summer not even finding out the answers to any of that. The fantasy was better. I was a hot mess express, but the fantasy world felt so nice as things with Jeff were so bad and the kids were literally without a dad.

There was nothing about me that would have attracted this guy to me. I came to practice every day with Ryan in a stroller. A woman with two kids under five, and even though I wasn't wearing a ring, there was no real reason to be sure I was single. Plus, he's the coach and I'm a parent of one of his kids. Totally inappropriate.

I was reentering the dating world, and if we're being honest, I was entering it for the first time ever. Jeff and I met when I was twenty. I'd never dated as an adult. And I had so much to learn and needed so much practice. The first thing I needed to do was give a guy my number, something I'd never done in my life unsolicited.

Swim Coach and I talked every now and then at practice, but that was it. And when the season ended, I knew it was now or never to get brave on this dating thing and see if there was any possibility with him. And since I still didn't know if he was single, I refused to put myself out there if I wasn't sure. So, I bit the bullet and sent a message to one of the team moms and swore her to secrecy that I asked.

He's single! And quite the eligible bachelor from what I hear! Not even seeing anyone right now, He's a teacher at the high school—and I hear all the kids at school love him and the swim team kids all really like him too.

I woke up to that message at 12:15AM and was so giddy that suddenly I was wide awake. And I stayed up for almost THREE hours. I was so mad I couldn't sleep, but I kept practicing what I'd say to him and playing out his reaction. And every time I played it in my head, it was a positive response. Never once did I practice being embarrassed. Probably would have chickened out if I had.

I still feel silly for feeling so hopeful and for hanging on to this Coach crush for more than two months, and I felt crazier for trusting God to bring me a father for my kids and a partner for me, and that he's going to do it quickly so they don't suffer. How could I be that blessed? I don't deserve to meet *the one* on the first try. But that small voice in my head that is the eternal optimist wonders if I am that lucky, if I am that blessed. Could Swim Coach be for me? Would he be willing to date someone with two kids? I really had no idea.

And then, I found another person who knew him from work. It had been a few years, but she said the girls swooned over him, and he came across as pretty cocky and full of himself. I was disappointed to admit that I could absolutely see that about him, and it made me wonder if I'd just been putting him up on a pedestal.

Since the meets and practices were over, my last chance to see him was at our awards banquet. I looked hot. My hair behaved. My makeup was simple but flawless. And my outfit was casual cool and also really sexy. This made me confident that I'd know immediately if Swim Coach wanted me kids and all, or if they were too much for him.

Peyton picked *that night* to suddenly be really clingy to him and kept hitting him on the butt and following him around. That did NOT make things easier for me, but I guess it's a step up from her being mean to him or crying around him—both of which happened that summer. (*Why was I thinking there was any chance this guy would want to date me after dealing with my emotional mess of a four-year-old all summer while I sat on the sidelines with a two-year-old in a stroller?*)

After handing out awards, I got a bit worried I'd missed my chance to get him on his own. Alas, (no such) luck was on my side, and the other coaches got up and he was at the table mostly alone. So, I went over and took an open seat at the end of the table. Mostly, I stuck to my script, but I'm sure not quite as cool as in my rehearsals. I thanked him and congratulated him on doing such a great job with all the little kids this year, and then I went for it.

"I have no idea if you're single or not, but I am. And now that it's the end of the season, I just wanted to let you know that I would be interested in going out sometime. You seem like a really great guy, and I'd love to do that if you're interested."

There was lots of smiling and nodding through this, but he didn't say anything AT ALL. Actual silence. I handed him my number even though he didn't ask for it, so I knew he didn't want it. But he was kind to my brave soul and said, "Thank you."

And I said, "Okay" or something stupid and got up and left!

Ughhhhh. It was so painful and embarrassing, but really, it went smoothly as far as rejections could go. I could pretend to be positive and think he was just caught off guard and would call me in a few days. But I got the reality check I needed, and I knew he had no interest in dating someone with two kids. And that's totally fair. It was also the scary reality I was now in. He successfully avoided me and kept his distance the rest of the evening.

I left with an entirely new appreciation for men doing the asking all the time. It's unbearably awkward and nerve-wracking. And when we walk around in packs or even have one friend with us, hell no. With the tables turned, I'd never walk over to a guy and ask him out or give him my number if there was someone else nearby to watch me stumble!

A few days went by, and the rejection started sweeping through me. I hadn't slept well the night of the rejection, and it was just

153

in my face what a hard uphill battle I was facing. I didn't care about Swim Coach, but that was my first dose of the reality of my future. While watching *The Bachelorette* that night, I got on to eHarmony. Then Match. Whoa, these sites seemed expensive. No way would I pay to do this, right? But I was willing to try out the free version of eHarmony.

On that one, you can connect with all the matches you want and talk to them... but you can't see their pictures. And of the few guys I started talking to, I was really intrigued. The conversation topics the site gives are awesome and so easy, and helpful to dive into the inner workings of people. And I was hooked. I lasted a full forty-eight hours before I needed to see the faces of these guys, so I bit the bullet and signed up for twelve months.

I'd seen one of the eHarmony guys pop up on Hinge, another dating site that connects you to people through a "six degrees of separation" connection, and he looked normal, so I was willing to give this all a try.

Suddenly, I was in deep talks with four guys, shocked that I would potentially have four dates on the horizon. I'm pretty sure I'd never been on four real dates in my life, much less with four different guys. It felt hot and fun and entertaining. But would I feel that way in five years? In five months? Would I feel this way if I didn't already have everything I want and need with Peyton and Ryan?

My best friend Katie was right. Online dating is a full-time job if you're doing it right. There are so many potential people to get to know. And what I loved about eHarmony is that it only shows people who meet my "must have" qualifications and ideally all of my other requirements, but it will venture out for things that weren't must haves. For example, it was a must have that they be non-smokers. But it was important that they have no kids and had never been married, but I was willing to look at them if we had enough in common.

Over the course of two weeks, I managed to line up four dates. That's when I learned how flakey people are when it comes to online dating. One by one, I got a text message asking to reschedule. They all seemed believable, but I quickly realized this is pretty normal in the online dating world, and people just disappear. Maybe they decided to see someone else exclusively? Or decided they actually didn't want to go on a date with someone with kids? Or I lived too far to make it worthwhile? Who knows? I ended up canceling one myself because I had to take my daughter to the doctor, and then we didn't get around to rescheduling. I tried saving my most promising date so it would be the last of the four, allowing me time to practice, and then he ended up being my first!

My first date in thirteen years. Through some Facebook stalking, I'd found out we had a few friends in common, so I was feeling relaxed and more excited for the date. And. It. Went. Great. Conversation was easy. He was cute. And I was really interested in a second date. I had a blast, and it made me feel really hopeful not just for him, but for dating in general.

The only awkward part of the evening was when he asked about Jeff. He asked if we were still married or if he had much time with the kids.

I didn't give him any details, but told him, "No, he's not a part of their lives."

It was a hard balance because this divorce was a huge part of where I was in life, but it's not *who* I was in life. I didn't want Jeff to define me. I also quickly realized after dating this guy a few times that talking about my ex wasn't the best way to get to know someone or for them to get to know me. Rookie mistake.

My date went to the beach for a long weekend after our first date so a second one had to wait. He texted me from his vacation though. I found myself checking my phone waiting to hear from him.

While I didn't want to play any games, I also didn't want to appear clingy. I decided that I'd done my part to give him confidence that I was interested in a second date, so I chose to cool it and wait for him. And the waiting sucked.

It also gave me all this time to think about how I could actually *have* a relationship. I wanted to date, but I also wanted to parent. And I wanted to be a *great* parent. Figuring out how to see him more than once a week without him interacting with the kids didn't even seem like it made sense or could be possible. I couldn't imagine how it would work.

The following week, I had date #2 with this guy. It was awkward. Like, uncomfortably awkward. It was like I was on a date with my brother. He wasn't great at asking me a ton of questions, and I felt like I had to keep pulling things out of him.

He said he'd never in a relationship longer than six months (we were both in our thirties), but he didn't elaborate more than that. My friend has this theory that all men make a decision at six months of whether to keep dating or break it off. I shared that with him, and he laughed and said he never really thought about it, that maybe it was subconscious.

He'd been irritating me leading up to the date because we basically planned on Sunday that we'd go out on Tuesday, and I didn't get a message from him until almost 11PM on Monday, and it didn't even mention the date. A red flag for flakiness went up.

Then we went straight from work (at my request) and got Mexican, a cheap and naturally quick service meal. We were done dinner around 6:15 and instead of trying to prolong the date, he said, "Well I'm sure your kids want to see their mom and have you put them to bed."

What???

So, he walked me to my car (a positive), we had an awkward hug, and he said he'd be in touch about this weekend.

I hadn't even gotten home before I got two texts:

"Thanks again for coming to dinner."

Then a few minutes later,

"Sorry I was a little quiet."

That was weird, so I actually called him on the phone. I told him that I couldn't get a read on him.

He said, "Yeah, I've heard that before. It's well-documented."

Okay, so potentially this was why you're single? You don't want to open up?

But then I also felt the need to address him shoo-ing me home. I texted him:

"So for the record, unless it's because you don't want to hang out, I don't need to be home to put my kids to bed. They're in good hands with my mom or dad! I know the idea of a single mom is weird, so I get it either way."

He responded that he just wasn't sure how to handle it even though he'd dated a single mom before. I decided to leave it alone unless he pursued things. I thought he'd be polite enough to let me know either way.

While waiting to see if date #3 would happen, I had a first (and last) date with another guy. Bless his heart. He was very sweet but so nerdy and awkward. I was happy we'd met at a Panera Bread over my lunch break and that was all.

After I left, I had to send the awkward text: "I wasn't feeling the connection, but you seem really great… best of luck."

Two-date guy continued to text me throughout the week, but it was always so vague, and it made me feel like he was just keeping me waiting in the wings in case something didn't work out with another girl he was seeing. Otherwise, it didn't make sense to waste his time reaching out to me if he didn't want to date someone with kids.

But it continued to give me time to think. And now, as I ventured into the dating world post-divorce, I realized that not only did I have to wow a man about *me*, but my kids would have to wow him too. I'd have to get him to love me THREE times. Talk about tough odds. Not that people don't love my kids, but would they want to step up and be a parent to my kids? That's an entirely new ballgame.

We went out one more time. It was the day after I'd received word that my divorce was official and the judge had signed off on it.

For our third date, we met at his house and I brought a six pack and had him give me a tour of his place. We went out to dinner, and when we got back to his place, I invited myself in since he didn't suggest it. Maybe he was just that shy? But then he didn't offer me a drink or sit down or anything.

As we ended the night, I went in for another awkward hug. And then he caught me off guard by kissing me. A totally standard first date kiss that I wasn't prepared for at all and thus didn't get to enjoy.

It felt like kissing my hand, and I was pissed. I thought it was just an "I'm going to be polite" kiss and that he wasn't interested—because why else do you boot a girl out of your house at 9PM on a Friday night?

I went home and just let it be. He'd totally fallen in to friend zone, but I was enjoying the dating practice and if he'd been interested, I would have gone out again. But he didn't feel anything either. Such a standup guy though—he had the decency to be totally honest and tell me that over the phone. Even with my limited dating knowledge, I know this was a rarity.

I hope by now he's found someone because he seemed like a really solid guy.

Chapter 17

Me again

If you're reading this book, then there's a good chance you've read *Carry On, Warrior* or *Love Warrior* by Glennon Doyle. Her first book came into my life exactly when I needed it, and ever since, I've been hooked on her words. At the time, she actively maintained a blog and shared her hilarious parenting struggles and eventually opened up about her marital struggles as well.

She was one of those women who felt like she knew exactly how I felt. And she'd been through so much tough stuff and still had this aura of joy and optimism—something I was working so hard to maintain. As a recovering alcoholic, I'd looked at her as this picture of success. Someone who hit rock bottom and managed to make it out the other side, with this beautiful, wonderful life.

And for some reason, she was coming to speak at a free event at my local library. Me and my fellow single mom girlfriends were the first to sign up for tickets. The event even included free childcare, and I was over-the-moon excited to meet her and have her love on me and the kids.

Since she's originally from Virginia, like me, I got to meet her family too. Sister, Bubba, and Tish! And she told stories. A lot of her talk was stuff from her book, but hearing her speak put it in a new context. And there was more. So much more. I wish I'd recorded the whole thing.

"Life only gets easier when we stop pretending it's not hard."

I don't know if Glennon was the originator of that quote, but it was one of my key takeaways from the night. My life had been hard the last couple of years, and I knew it. For some crazy reason though, that quote is true. Once I was able to accept everything happening to and around me, I was better able to deal with it. And once I was better able to deal with it, it became more manageable. It became easier.

I'd had my heart broken, and I was trying to find my way back out of the dark. That night, Glennon talked about the *broken-hearted* and how everyone who does anything for a cause—it all stems from having a broken heart. From being at that rock bottom. This made so much sense to me, because all I want to do now is help other moms in my boat. Help others who are dealing with the aftermath of addiction. Glennon says we should rush towards our *broken-heartedness* and embrace it, so we can use that pain to help others.

She says the pain is required, but the suffering—that's optional.

———— ◆ ————

A few weeks after that event, on our way to church, Peyton, my sweet little four-year-old, said to me, "Mommy, my heart is breaking."

She said her heart was breaking because she didn't see her daddy.

I was in tears most of the service thinking about her. And then thinking about myself. And if dating was right for me.

I decided the answer was yes. I was whole again and healed. It's my children who were not.

But me dating can only help as far as I can see. What if I never find them a man to be a father figure to them? What if Jeff never sees them again? What if he does but it's once every six months? I couldn't bare their pain.

After church, I told Peyton I prayed for her in my service.

"Why?" she asked.

"Because you told me your heart was breaking, and that made me sad."

"Yes, my heart is broken. I can feel it. (touching her heart) Because my daddy is gone. It's gonna be broken for a long time."

Tears were springing to my eyes, and I was just at a loss for how to respond. Finally, the words came to me. "It won't be broken forever. You'll be okay."

As we drove home, Peyton played in the back with her stuffed animal, oblivious to my silent sobs from the front seat.

Children don't want to make their parents sad, so if she was going to be honest with me, and then saw me cry, I was afraid she'd stop opening up. And that's not what I want. So, I just let it be. I couldn't offer her the right words at the time, but I told her I loved her, and we went to the playground on our way home. She was brave and happy. So, I was too.

———————◆———————

Sometimes, I take for granted how strong I was to leave. How strong my friends were to leave. Especially all of the stay at home moms. It was hard to do but such an easy decision too. I had to put my kids first. Doing what's best for them meant leaving NOW.

Leaving isn't easy, but I think we just know in our hearts when it's the right thing to do. I knew the repercussions of my decision, and now I was living them out to the best of my abilities and with the best tribe I could muster.

Work had been getting in my way recently though. I noticed I'd been teetering on tears for a couple of weeks now. I couldn't shake my emotions, and I couldn't figure out why I suddenly felt so sad.

Because I was so emotional, I couldn't tell if the way I was feeling at work was a rational or irrational feeling. I couldn't tell if I was doing well or if I sucked at my job. And I couldn't tell what my boss and peers thought either. I felt like I was constantly being judged and criticized and it had started taking its toll.

And then on top of that, I felt like my financial stability was literally burning away. Peyton going to kindergarten was the milestone I'd been waiting for—where I was suddenly supposed to be breaking even, able to start possibly saving again, and certainly not supposed to be draining my savings every month.

Then our dog died suddenly.

Then I had to pay for the plane tickets for our upcoming Disney trip.

And then... I found out that Jeff lost his job.

I assumed he was fired, and of course he never had the decency to tell me. I first noticed something was off when his child support was short by thirteen dollars. No big deal though, right? He probably just didn't work forty hours, and there's a max to the percent of his check I can take.

But then next time, no money came. HR couldn't tell me if he was employed, so I called the kitchen myself and asked for him. The guy who answered said he no longer worked there. And he hadn't for about a month.

I texted Jeff and asked him how he was planning on paying me without a job since I'm sure he didn't feel like going back to jail (*it's not that easy, FYI, to send someone to jail for not paying child support, but he didn't know that*). And I was shocked to actually get a text back:

Don't worry I'll go to the bank tomorrow and get a check for you don't worry.

Don't threaten me about going back to jail

I had no idea if he would actually send me money, but man I hoped so. My friend, who is a seasoned pro at this, told me that I should consider child support a bonus and never to depend on it. Wish I'd known that sooner.

I started to consider a town house, something cheaper so I didn't have these financial fears that I was constantly dealing with. I had a lot of equity in my house, so if I sold it and bought something cheaper, I could put myself in a better financial situation. It was hard to be that humble though. It felt like accepting defeat, like I couldn't make it. I wanted so desperately to keep my kids in the same home and not uproot them. But at what cost?

It took me another two or three weeks to let necessity overcome my pride. I called my realtor and told her there was a townhouse

I wanted to see. It was in my neighborhood, so no school change, and the same pool in the summer.

The place was really nice, and the price was great. I needed a few days to think about it, and obviously would need to get my house ready to sell first anyway.

After the kids were in bed that night, I was lying in bed when I heard Peyton stirring in her room. She sounded awake so I peeked in, and sure enough, she was sitting in her bed sobbing. I went in her room and she was crying so hard and had wet the bed. I couldn't do anything to calm her. I thought maybe she was still asleep so I tried slapping her cheeks a few times. Nothing would calm her. I tried covering her mouth, squeezing her, shushing in her ear. Nothing could calm her cries. Finally, I asked her if she wanted to go down and get a scoop of ice cream, and that did it. Ice cream apparently works at all ages when you're sad.

She was never able to articulate why she was crying—if she had a bad dream, or if something hurt. But she did tell me she wanted her daddy. She asked when he was coming back.

And then she said, "He's a joker."

When I asked her what she meant, she said, "Well, when he talks to me on the phone, he says he's going to come, but he makes a joke. He never comes. He's just joking."

Wow, she'd learned it. We can't rely on him.

Chapter 18

Everything changes

It would have been our nine-year anniversary. The noteworthy day didn't even make me sad. I spent the first part of my morning deleting its history on Facebook so it wouldn't keep showing up in my Timehop every year.

Then, shortly before 10pm, I got a call from Jeff's brother, Chris. I answered happily, assuming he was calling to check in and see how I was doing given the day's significance. Instead, he spit out news that I honestly couldn't have predicted for another twenty years:

Jeff was dead.

Like, actually dead. Heart stopped beating, dead. I really couldn't believe it, and I needed more proof for it to sink in.

His fiancée found him—yes, that girl he'd been sneaking around with was legit engaged to him. Never mind the fact that it happened after three months of dating and while she was still married to someone else.

She got home at 9:30PM and found him dead. She'd been messaging him throughout the day, and their texting stopped early evening. She had to find Chris through Facebook because Jeff had kept his family so hidden from her, and she didn't know how to reach out to anyone. That was how their introduction went—her having to call him and tell him that his brother had died.

After I hung up with Chris, I called my parents and told them. We were all in shock. What was there to say? My emotions were all over the place.

Sad because the man I loved was an alcoholic and managed to die from it at only thirty-six years old. And sad for the kids who now had no hope of knowing their dad.

Relieved that I had a resolution to our saga. I didn't have to wait and wonder if he was going to be a part of their lives as they got older, always letting them down.

And then **guilt** for feeling relieved. So much guilt.

As I sat on my bed trying to process everything, I got another phone call. This one was from the police on scene at their apartment.

Before he could even tell me that Jeff was dead, I asked, "So it's true?"

Then I said "f*ck" to the cop. I couldn't believe it. He asked when I'd last seen Jeff and if I had any reason to suspect foul play.

I told him that I hadn't seen him in months, and he was an alcoholic. I assumed that was to blame but told him I couldn't know anything for certain.

It wasn't until later that I wondered why the cops called me to tell me the news. We weren't married anymore. There's nothing with the police that would have listed me as a next of kin. Turns out that because there'd been a previous protection order against him that it likely triggered a phone call.

Chris and I called and texted a few more times throughout the night, neither of us sleeping. Apparently, Jeff was found lying on the floor by the couch with her dog by his side. The EMT assumed he fell off the couch at some point after passing out, so he likely died in his sleep, thankfully.

It would be weeks before the medical examiner's report would come back, but his cause of death was officially listed as alcoholism. His BAC was .39. To put that into perspective, the legal limit to drive in most states is 0.08. A sloppy drunk is around 0.16-20. (University 2019)

All night long, I cried off and on. I was really sad at the finality of everything and knowing I'd never get an apology, never get my real Jeff back, never see him with the kids again. But mostly, I felt relief. And then I hated myself for feeling relief. One of my biggest fears was always the unknown—would Jeff be in and out of our lives, constantly causing issues for us? Would he get better and we could be civil and friendly? Could he ever apologize and truly repent for everything caused by his addiction? Then the unknowns for me—would child support keep coming? Would I need to move? Would I be able to afford college? And now suddenly, I know all of those answers. And it was peaceful.

Since sleep wasn't coming, I went into planning mode. I emailed Peyton's school counselor and also my church. I started thinking about how I could honor Jeff at his memorial service, what I could do to help the kids remember him. It was overwhelming. I decided that the answer for now was to focus on the next right thing—the right thing for me, for the kids, and for Jeff's family.

The next morning, I hopped online and pinged my one poor co-worker who was at work early, and I told him the news so he could share with our manager. Said I'd be in touch when I knew more but not to expect me in for the rest of the week. I got Peyton on the school bus and Ryan off to daycare, like it was just a regular day.

Her school counselor called, and I told her I'd keep her in the loop as things developed. I didn't plan on telling Peyton yet. Not until the school week was over.

My next stop was my church. The place that had been my safe haven for the last year and a half. I had developed in my faith so deeply during this brokenhearted time, and even though it was a church of twenty-five hundred members, I knew the pastors and they knew me. Two of them greeted me with open arms and tissues as soon as I stepped in the office.

I sat on the couch with Pastor Paul and told him and Pastor Marie that my overwhelming feeling was guilt. It wasn't just the guilt from feeling relief; I was afraid that I had prayed for this to happen.

Of course, I never actually prayed that he would die, but what I constantly prayed for was finality. I wanted him in, or I wanted him out. I was so fearful of him ping ponging in and out of our lives over the years and causing the kids so much distress, sadness, and embarrassment. I prayed for God to let it go one way or the other, not both.

Pastor Paul referenced Romans 8:28

And we know that God causes everything to work together for the good of those who love God and are called according to his purpose for them. (NLT)

I struggled with understanding that verse for a long time. God wanted to answer my prayer because I loved Him? What about all the other people who love Him? Who don't get their prayers answered? And why was my struggle so short? Some people pray for years and never get what they're looking for. And Jeff dying wasn't even what I was looking for, but it *was* an answer.

As I took a step back and time passed, I realized that Jeff was never going to get better. God knows how our lives play out. He knew. If there'd been a chance, I think Jeff would still be here today. But there was no hope for his recovery, and because of that, God ended his suffering *and ours* sooner rather than later. Out of our lives was the answer God gave me. And in the most permanent way.

And Jeff dying on our anniversary. I take that really personally. But not in a negative way. Despite the horrible way Jeff treated me in his last year, I know he adored me. He loved me so much, and I truly believe that the day of our anniversary, he was feeling particularly sad and reminiscent. I believe he drank the day away as he often did, but this time, his "one more" bourbon ended up as one too many. He died that day of a broken heart.

Going to see my pastors is something I really cherish to this day. Having them there to provide comfort and answers. It's not something I ever envisioned for myself, and even though we've moved on to a new church, that place and those people will forever have a special place in my heart. Being with the grieving and saying the right things takes a really special person.

After we talked through my conflicting emotion, I told them how nervous I was to tell Peyton, not knowing how she'd react. Marie gave me a "memory box" to give to her. A small box with strips of colored paper inside. It was a place for us to write down her memories, so she'd always hold on to them. It was perfect. Peyton and I wrote various memories together for a long time. She added photos and drawings, and as she learned to write more, she put her own things inside.

174

It was a Friday afternoon, and I knew that after school, with the full weekend ahead, I'd tell her the truth. I had previously scheduled time to go to her classroom and volunteer, so I kept that commitment. Spending the time with her at school was almost too much. She was so happy and excited to show me off to her friends. I helped her classmates with stations around the room, working on letter recognition and counting games.

My cousin met me at the house that afternoon so she could take care of Ryan while I told Peyton the news.

She asked for a snack, and I decided right now, with Cheetos, would be the best time to tell her. So, I told her I needed to tell her something and we sat down in our cozy chair together.

First, let me back up a moment. Six weeks earlier, on Labor Day, our dog had gotten sick overnight, and I took her to the vet as soon as the kids were up. She was only eight years old but had a history of vomiting without cause. This time, it was different, and she was clearly struggling. Almost immediately, the vet came to see me and told me that our dog was very unstable and they may not be able to save her. They gave her oxygen and ran blood tests. Her red blood cell count came back at only 6%—when it should be at 35%. This suggested some immune attack on her system. She also had a heart murmur and the vet thought there may be some heart failure going on.

My neighbor brought Peyton over to the vet's office, so she could be there to say goodbye. It was so sudden, and she could barely process what was happening. I told her that our dog wouldn't be coming home with us, and she immediately started crying and getting upset. It took a while to calm her down.

I asked her to be brave, and through her tears she said, "But I don't want to be brave."

We went into another room and they brought our sweet pup to us. She looked like she was just resting. On a doggy bed and covered with a blanket. She had a port in her leg to give her meds, but it didn't look like an IV, so that was good. We petted her and then I picked her up to let Peyton hold her. Then she peed on me, and we had a laugh. I thought she actually died then the way her tongue was hanging out of her mouth, so I had the doctor come in. Peyton watched as she gave the medicine to put her down. We told Peyton it was food and water to help the dog feel better. And just like that, she was going to go to Heaven. She kept saying she didn't want her to go to Heaven, that she wanted her to be home with us. It was awful and so sad.

We went home, her collar and paw print in hand, and looked at pictures of her and talked about all the fun things she could do in Heaven. I told Peyton that she could talk to her any time and that she'd see her in her dreams. All day long, she went outside yelling her name and talking to the clouds.

At bedtime, we talked about her seeing our dog in her dreams.

That was Peyton's first experience with death, and six weeks later, I was so grateful for it.

———————— ◆ ————————

"Peyton, you know how Daddy hasn't been to visit you and I told you that I didn't know if he'd come back again? Well, he's not going to be able to come visit you anymore. Daddy died this week."

She cried and sat in my lap saying she wanted to see him, that she wanted him to come see her.

She said, "Daddy doesn't love me anymore."

I immediately reassured her that he loved her so much and was looking over her from Heaven. She wanted to see him, so I told her to pull out one of our family albums. She pulled out the year she was born, and we sat down and looked at pictures. We talked through our "Inside Out" emotions (the movie had come out earlier that year and was my life saver at getting her to express how she was feeling) and when we looked at each picture, either of Jeff or of her as a baby, I asked her what emotion was happening in the picture. She liked that game a lot—especially the baby pictures of her screaming or laughing.

A few pages into the book, she remembered her Cheeto balls and put the bowl in her lap, eating them one by one. We went through the whole book, and then my cousin arrived with Ryan. I told her what we were doing and then asked Peyton what emotion she was feeling right now.

"Joy!" she said.

Oh, melt my heart you strong and darling girl. She was happy the rest of the night.

Before we went to bed, I reminded her of the memory box that Marie from church made her. We wrote down a few happy memories—she couldn't name anything specific (just, "My daddy loves me so much") so I put a few in there to start. She wanted to write her memories too, which was her writing "DADDY" and a bunch of hearts. Then I had her write Daddy and Peyton on the top of the box. She said she wanted to sleep with it in the bed that night.

His brother's family came and stayed with us that next week, and it was so wonderful having them at the house. Chris had the hard job of handling the cremation. I really needed to see Jeff and have some time to talk to him once more and was really thankful for that opportunity.

It was devastatingly sad to see him lying on the cot, his hair shaggy and so much grayer than six months earlier. I got a closer look at the giant tattoo he'd put on his leg that Spring—a cougar, I think. Maybe a panther.

I told him how angry I was at him for being so selfish and careless with his life. I told him that I hated how his kids would never know him, but I was grateful that it was because he was dead and not because he was gallivanting around living some brand new life without them.

I tried to make one of those handprint impressions for the kids and his mom, which the cremation place was kind enough to do.

Only, I learned that your extremities swell after death, so it didn't even work that well.

There are also a ton of things you can order to help you remember the deceased. I ordered a necklace for Peyton and a keychain with Jeff's thumb print for Ryan—a reminder to be safe on the road and make good decisions.

The whole week was a whirlwind. So many revelations came out, and since Jeff had been so secretive living this life with his girlfriend, bombs just kept on dropping. We didn't think our jaws could go any lower. And worst of all, Jeff's parents didn't want to give him a funeral. They didn't think anyone would come. I was furious and hurt for him and volunteered to pay for the whole thing. He was thirty-six years old. Of course people would want to come and pay their respects.

It was during this time, we found out that Jeff had been engaged to Sara, the girl who found him. She was (is) married and had an affair with Jeff before leaving her husband. Their first date was the day after I declined the offer to go with him to the Valentine's party at daycare.

They snuck around for a month in hotel rooms, where I'm sure he blew through the entire $10,000 I'd given him as buy out for the house. She was so blind to his ways and probably thought he was full of money, despite being a line cook making less than fifteen dollars an hour.

They moved in together shortly after and were engaged by the beginning of June. They'd gone shopping for rings, and she picked out a ring that was $6000, which he paid for entirely on credit. He didn't have $6,000 to spend on a ring, or anything. I'd love to believe she had no idea he was completely broke, but I don't know.

Sara said she had no idea how secretive he was, didn't know he was drinking again for a long time. But in July, a month after they'd gotten engaged, it all fell apart. He always had a drink in his hand.

When he lost his job, I think that was it. He'd spent the last two months literally drinking himself to death. The week before he died, Sara told Jeff's brother that he had been very yellow—jaundiced. Signs of liver failure. And although she suggested he go to a doctor, he refused, and she didn't have the knowledge or conviction to force him. After he died and they were cleaning up his things, Sara found a duffle bag full of empty whiskey bottles. She was as clueless as I had been.

There were very few things of his I asked his family for, but one was his cell phone so that I could make it a kid phone for the kids to use. Sara didn't delete their texting history before returning it, and it was like a soap opera. I just couldn't stop reading—even though a ton of it was either sexting or about their sex life. It was disgusting, and the entire relationship was so unhealthy.

One time, he was staying at a hotel and Sara came over. He must've passed out before she arrived, and there were countless pissed off texts from her asking where he was and how she really appreciated sitting outside a hotel late at night!

Oh honey, you have no clue what kind of life you were setting yourself up for... I told you, soap opera. I couldn't stop reading these things.

They disagreed over his guns too. She hated them, and he wasn't allowed to stay with her unless he got a safe or sent them to his parents'. Sara claimed to Chris that she begged him to see his kids and call them, but every time she did, he'd get in a rage and say he'd do it on his terms. Like he'd told me the last time we spoke, on Ryan's birthday.

Yes, she was with Jeff in his final months of destruction and she probably did try to help. But she was selfish and blindly in lust or love. She didn't understand that his life was with us, not her. He was an imposter while he was with her. She kept saying that she was fighting for what he wanted, and that's where I'd really get offended. Because she didn't know what he wanted. She didn't even know him. Not the real him. If he's really in Heaven and pure and perfect now, then he's our Jeff again. The one before his cousin's death all those years earlier. The one who was here most of the time before his downfall. And he loves **me**. He loves the kids.

The funeral was the following weekend. A couple days prior, I went and met with the pastor of the church where it was held. Jeff had been attending back when we first separated, and the pastor had gotten to know him.

She and I talked a lot about Jeff's time at the church. He went to both Sunday services. Came in his suit every week. Had question after question for her about Jesus. Jeff was baptized as a baby, and he began to explore his faith—even for a short time.

I have to believe in Jesus' promises that God is merciful, and our sins are forgiven. God, I know, does not punish someone because of an addiction or weakness, so I believe that God did not punish him for the way he behaved or for his heart that he was drowning in alcohol.

That whole week, before I felt sure he was in Heaven, I could sense Jeff's presence when I was standing and singing to Ryan at bedtime. Because of course he'd be there. With the boy he never got a chance to know. With the sweet and innocent boy who didn't know a single mistake his daddy made.

The day of the funeral, my parents came over and picked up me and the kids. Ryan, just two years old, looked so adorably handsome in his first shirt and tie combo.

Peyton was a doll baby in her dress and cardigan and Princess Belle shoes I gave her. This was going to be a special day, and she wanted to feel like a little princess. I'd told her the day would be really fun and a way to remember her dad, and she'd get to see a ton of family.

We got to the church and the kids shot off to the nursery to start exploring new toys. Our friends and family started arriving.

They'd take one look at the kids and immediately put their hand to their heart, like "Oh, those poor children."

The kids were so young and clueless though. This was the greatest day ever. Every aunt or friend brought them little gifts—stuffed animals, books, lollipops. Everyone wanted to love on them.

Ryan was overwhelmed by it all and clung to me. The whole time, he wouldn't let me put him down. It was already a stressful day, so this increased my sweat level ten-fold!

But I felt beautiful in the green dress I spent forever hunting for—the exact shade of Jeff's favorite color. Since I'd had the week off from work to get things in order, I was able to go from store to store trying on dresses and trying to decide, "What exactly does one wear to their ex-husband's funeral?"

The dress made me feel even better when Sara showed up with her mom. Thank God she had enough sense not to sit in the family section of seats with us. I never met her. And she didn't wear her ring. Everything I learned about her was through Chris's few conversations with her and her elicit texting history.

I was the only person to speak at the service. On the car ride up, I sat in the very back—behind the kids in their car seats. I had the speech printed out and I kept reading it over and over tweaking words here and there and trying to practice reading the entire thing without crying.

When it was my turn to go up, I put down the Spiderman stuffed animal that I'd been holding for Ryan and sat it down next to its new owner.

Jeff's parents were so nervous about what I'd say in my eulogy, but I had to be honest and true to Jeff's tragic end. I got up there and realized I'd forgotten a tissue, so no pressure, but now I really needed to make it through this thing in one piece. My voice cracked, and I couldn't look up at a single person because they were all crying. Even my brother, who I'm really not sure I've ever seen cry.

"First, let me say thank you for being here. Thank you for being here to remember the real Jeff, the one we all knew and loved for so long before alcohol began consuming his life…

He told me he loved me after about three dates, and I shot him down and told him he did not. But that was Jeff—Always impulsive and not the brightest crayon in the box. But what he lacked there, he made up for in heart, kindness, and humor. And he kept me fed…

I've been asked a lot over the last year and a half why I didn't carry anger or hate in my heart for this situation, and the answer is quite simply a combination of my faith and my understanding of alcoholism. This disease truly changed the brain chemistry of the man I loved and the great dad I saw, and he became a new person. That new person is not who I'm up here remembering today. That's not the person our children will hear about as they grow up. And I don't think it's who you'll remember either. But I do hope that the lessons we've all learned going through this experience is something you can pay forward."

After I finished and the service concluded, we went into the fellowship hall and his slideshow I made played on repeat. I was nervous to share too much or too little or the wrong things. I was afraid his family would place blame on me. I was sometimes afraid it was all too much, but Jeff's two aunts, who I'd never met, just hugged and loved me and told me how strong I was and how thankful they were that Jeff had me to look out for him. It was reassurance that it took a lot of strength to stand up to an alcoholic and force that person to figure out their own fate, without enabling him.

I didn't speak to his parents the entire time we were at the church, but when I saw them at dinner that evening, they both thanked me for my speech. I hope they meant it.

◆

Once I made it through the funeral, it was time to get back to reality. I had to go back to work, and that was really strange. For the last 18 months, only a very small group of people knew anything I'd been going through. I didn't want anyone to know, and then when Jeff died, suddenly they all knew. People were so kind for a while. It helped.

At the same time, I also had to deal with the business of dying. His parents and brother graciously let me be the administrator of Jeff's estate. Since he didn't really have any assets anyway, and whatever he did have would go to the kids, this helped simplify the process a lot.

I learned a lot about the courts and laws as it relates to death without a will. The most important, and relieving thing, I learned is that when a person dies, their debts generally die with them. So that $6000 ring that wasn't paid for, she could keep it. I was really annoyed about it for a while, but I didn't have to pay for it. And that poor girl had to find him dead in her apartment and call 9-1-1. That could have been me, and I thank God every day that it wasn't.

I learned that because I was no longer his wife, I needed to carry paperwork everywhere that designated me as the administrator of his estate so that people would talk to me and give me information. He had taken out $10,000 from his retirement account just three days before he died, and he never cashed the check. It took months to straighten out and get the company to give me the money that rightfully belonged to the kids, and in the end, I only got it because I had a lawyer friend who helped me craft a letter using legal jargon and threatened them. The money came a week later.

I learned that when a parent dies, each child is eligible for social security benefits until they are eighteen. This was one of the biggest surprises for me! Even with Jeff's low salary, I was now getting over $2000 a month to help me with the kids. Comparatively, my child support had been less than $1000.

And most impactful, I learned my dad's financial forethought a week after Jeff and I separated would change our lives forever— he had Jeff sign over his life insurance policy to me. I made the $219 semi-annual payment just three times before he died. And two months later, I received the largest check of my life. A check that I immediately invested so I could have the kids' college paid for in the future. I used some over the next year to take my parents with me to Disney and to buy a new car for me and the kids. It really was Jeff's legacy to us.

Chapter 19

Moving forward

Even before Jeff died, I'd been planning a trip to Disney with the kids. One night while we were there, in the pool at Art of Animation, Peyton was playing with a little girl, whose dad was nearby. As Peyton and this little girl splashed around like new best friends, Peyton casually said, "Did you know my dad is in Heaven?"

And the girl's dad just had the best response—"Oh Mara, that's just like your grandma."

It doesn't seem like something I should remember, but in that moment, I thought tears may explode out of my eyes. It was such a sweet and thoughtful response. He made it so normal, and when he and I met eyes, I just felt so grateful for him.

It was natural for Peyton to talk about Jeff, like what happened was normal and no big deal. But it made others uncomfortable. What seemed natural for her was traumatic and sad for adults. Thankfully she didn't view his death that way. She *was* curious about him though.

One night, while baking Christmas cookies, she asked me about things I didn't like. I couldn't think of anything, and she said, "You hate cleaning the floors."

Why yes. Yes, I do. Then she asked me about things Daddy hated.

"Well, you know that Daddy was a chef, right? He liked to cook. But what he didn't like to do was bake cookies or make anything sweet! Daddy's so weird, huh?"

We ran through a list of things he hated—taking out the trash, baking, reading, eating lasagna at the beach, being on a schedule— especially on vacation, flying, spiders (terrified! I always killed them for him), me rubbing my cold feet against him in bed, my cold hands under his shirt purposely trying to give him the chills. In fact, he hated feet in general. I only got one foot rub while pregnant with Peyton, and not a single one with Ryan. I think he hated woodworking or doing anything with tools. He was gifted a fancy woodworking machine from his brother and parents and never used it. And any time repairs involved tools, he just wasn't into it. He wasn't a tinkerer, but then he could throw me for a loop and install car speakers for my birthday! He was terrible at math and spelling, which I think dyslexia was to blame there. And he hated when I would have him try to spell a word out before giving him the answer.

But the things he loved—the Steelers, Penguins, and talking about Pittsburgh. We went twice together and loved the city! If it wasn't so cold and snowy, I'd totally move there! He loved hockey and spent so much time watching it. He loved football, especially fantasy football, and he hated to lose—especially to his brother who ended up winning our league way more seasons than was fair! He loved chile rellenos when we got Mexican, and he got dirty martinis extra dirty with extra olives so I could eat the olives. He loved steak and seafood, and he talked about truffle oil like it was the holy grail of oils (I never noticed anything special when he used it!).

He was obsessed with World War II and the History and Military Channels. He wore cargo shorts all the time even though I constantly told him they weren't okay for grown men unless they were out in the wilderness!

He loved visors, even though he was balding in the back and I told him the visors probably didn't help! He loved to pamper his car and give it a good deep cleaning. And he had a Grateful Dead charm that he kept hanging from his rearview mirror for as long as I knew him. When I did my study abroad, he gave it to me to keep me safe since it was his good luck charm. Unfortunately, we never found it after he died. He loved Jimmy Buffet. That was the only musical overlap we had!

As I reached New Year's Eve and sat at home alone journaling, I couldn't believe how much my life changed in the last 365 days. I sat in my cozy chair with tears streaming down as I thought about the end of Jeff and what that meant for me and for the kids. And I knew that next year was going to be so much better for us.

This time last year, I was getting fifteen calls from Jeff begging me to talk to him and asking me what exactly he did wrong. After the 14th call, I answered and told him that all of these calls did not scream "sober" to me. Yet, always the victim, he just couldn't understand. "What did I do wrong? Why are you so mad at me?"

It was always about him, and how could someone be so mad at *him*? It was a horrible, horrible disease.

The year started with regular visits from Jeff. We refinanced the house just before his birthday, and he had his last visit with the kids just before my birthday. It was the first time I asked him to take a breathalyzer.

Peyton "graduated" from pre-k, and I sat looking out the window wondering if Jeff was going to show up. Instead, my parents filled the empty seat meant for him. After twelve months of separation, I filed the divorce papers, and it took until the end of the summer for the judge to sign. Never heard from him. Peyton even stopped asking for him by the time school started.

Then our anniversary and that call from his brother—where I thought he was just calling to check in on me. And he called to tell me *Jeff is dead.* The most surprising and, admittedly, relieving phone call. I was so sad and so happy for my children at the same time. This was what I prayed for, and I felt awful that it came to fruition—and so FAST! All I wanted was to have him get better, and I was sure that was going to happen. But if it wasn't, I asked God to spare the kids from that suffering and to keep us from the heartache.

This is just a better story for them. Now, they can just have happy memories of him, or hear about the good parts of him. Peyton already idolizes him and talks about him like he was this amazing, wonderful daddy.

As I tried to reenter the dating world, I really struggled with how to define myself. Part of me wanted to call myself a widow, but I don't think that's fair to my character and the decisions I made leading up to becoming a widow.

I'm divorced.

That's what I needed to put on those dating profiles. I'm divorced, and he's dead. He died less than two months after we divorced. On our anniversary. It was so confusing. I want to love him and honor him and share photos of us in love. But that's not how it would have been if he hadn't died. I struggled, and still do, with what's the right way to behave.

But I did love him, and I do miss him. I would often picture him in the kitchen or on the stairs or next to me in bed. It was hard.

All of my fears of running out of money were gone. I am so thankful to Jeff for that gift. That life insurance policy was his parting gift to me and the kids. Even the Social Security I received now is way more than he'd ever have been able to provide. These kids were so lucky, and the only thing that would make them luckier is if God could bless us with a man to be a dad to them.

I could only hope and pray that God hadn't given me all of my miracles and answered prayers already, and a good man was in my future.

———————◆———————

It had been four months since Jeff died, and we'd done pretty well settling into our peaceful life. Peyton still had emotional ups and downs though.

She'd say things like, "I don't want Daddy to be in Heaven. I want him right here—upstairs and downstairs."

She'd already forgotten that he didn't actually live here before he died. She told me she wanted to die and be in Heaven with him. (Four years later, this is still something she says on rare occasions.)

I still tell her that he wouldn't want that, and that we need her here with us—that she's not allowed to go until she's old. But then, she's smart enough to know that her daddy wasn't old and gray.

So why did he die? And he's *not here* with her, even when I tell her he's always here with her, invisible. That's not good enough for a five-year-old. She doesn't feel him, doesn't believe that he's with her. I never found the "right" way to help her through that. I just tried to listen and validate her feelings. There are lots of great children's books that address both death and being away from someone and I reference some I used at the end of this book.

And then when I thought it was already hard enough to know how to talk about death, she made it impossible.

"Mom, are you going to die too?"

I would never want to promise that I won't since I can't predict the future, so instead I told her, "We never know when we're going to die, but I hope to be here for a long time until I'm old and gray."

"What would happen to me and Ryan if you died?" she asked.

God, what a smart girl. She asked if she would move in with Cameron, our neighbor.

"No," I told her. "You'd go live with Nonnie and Pop Pop, and it would be so much fun. But I don't plan on going anywhere."

I tried so hard to find a way to focus on the positive, but she finally broke me, and I was crying as I told her, "I never want to leave you and Ryan."

She asked me a lot if she was going to have a new dad, and God willing, she would, but I honestly had no idea if I'd ever find someone good enough for all of us and I didn't know if I trusted myself or could give my life to someone again.

So instead, Peyton and I would talk about her two daddies in Heaven—God our father, and her daddy. I'd remind her that she was so lucky to have two daddies in Heaven who love her and look out for her.

———————◆———————

There are a lot of things that are hard about being a single parent. Sometimes, I would feel like I could never give them one hundred percent because I was so tired all the time. I relied on them to play with each other because I would be tired or bored after five minutes of hide and seek. But the hardest thing for me was not giving each the time and attention that I *wanted* to. I'm lucky though. My parents kept one child for a night almost every weekend, so I'd get to have extra one-on-one time with each kid.

Putting them to bed at night was always so rewarding. It's that moment where I successfully kept them alive for another day, and their little terror behavior was at bay for (hopefully) the next ten to twelve hours. And it's the time when I would remember how little they are and how breathtaking they look when they are sleeping so peacefully, and I can just stare away at them.

I looked at Peyton like that and wanted to just sit by her bed for another twenty minutes and cry or smile or close my eyes. But I couldn't. Because Ryan wasn't asleep yet. He was still learning to stay in his big boy bed and not leave his room.

So, I couldn't just sit in Peyton's room. And I couldn't just sit in Ryan's room for him to fall asleep first because it would take too long and Peyton would be waiting. Sure, I could go back in there after, but he was already peaceful and (mostly) content, so I didn't want to mess with the potential of him successfully putting himself to sleep. It had been six weeks and it had yet to happen—I had to lock his door every night, and then I go unlock it after he was asleep, and I'd find him pressed up against the door and have to push the door into him to get him to sit up or move so I could put him back in bed.

And bless his heart, he just could not stay in bed all night. After moving to a big boy bed, he got a cold and very quickly got accustomed to sleeping with mama when he woke up in the middle of the night. I'm a firm believer in not letting kids in the bed, yet with him, I was just too tired to keep putting him back in his room. And more fearful that he'd wake Peyton up and I'd have two of them to try and put back down at 3AM. This phase was really exhausting, and I could feel it taking a toll on my body.

I'd been doing the math recently, and with Ryan's latest sleep schedule, I was lucky if I got two uninterrupted hours of sleep at a time. And I was so restless anyway—waking up to every noise— that even when both kids are asleep, I'd find myself stirring. My under-eye circles had reached a stage five level of purple. It was terrible, and there was absolutely nothing I could do about it except remind myself that it's a phase, and in another year or two, they'd both be sleeping so much better.

But in the meantime, I tried relaxing my rule. Because honestly, I loved snuggling with him in bed, and he slept so peacefully with me. And even though I got about twelve inches of space in my king-sized bed, I didn't mind. I adore him more than I could ever put into words, and the way that little boy helped me when Jeff left, I just can't escape that feeling in my heart. He was my everything. He didn't face any of the heartache or confusion that Peyton did, and he was a helpless baby, not a three-nager little girl. He was my peace and my comfort, and his smile just breaks me every time I look at him.

Chapter 20

Meeting him

After taking a break from online dating, I started talking to a guy named Josh on eHarmony. I read through his profile, as usual, to decide if I wanted to respond to his questions, and the first thing I noticed was his blurry profile picture.

I never like to discount someone immediately due to one or two things I see on their profile, but I generally went with a 'three strikes and you're out' rule. A blurry profile picture definitely qualified as strike one.

Strike two on his profile was his job title, which he simply listed as "Construction." Now look, there's nothing wrong with anyone who works in construction, but after just getting out of a marriage to someone who was a restaurant cook and needed to rely on me financially, I just didn't want to take the risk of going down that road again. There was too much on my plate.

But that was it. Those were his two strikes. I couldn't find a third. I hadn't had the energy or time to devote to anyone for so long, but I figured I may be ready to try again. And after about a week of chatting through the site and texting, we had our first date.

Josh likes to tell the story that I was so desperate that I immediately messaged him back after he'd reached out online. And while it's true I was quick to respond to him, it had all been dumb luck. I usually logged on to eHarmony before I went to bed most nights, around 10PM, after the kids had gone to sleep. He'd sent me a message shortly before my usual log on time. I'm not one to play games, so why wouldn't I reply in the moment while I was already online?

I was generally anti-dinner for a first date because I never want to be stuck with someone for a whole meal if they aren't a good match. But I must have been craving some Bang Bang Shrimp that week.

For our first date, we went to Bonefish Grill. I got there first, maybe a few minutes early, and I think he was a few minutes late. It felt like an eternity watching people walk in and wondering who this blurry-faced guy would be.

We shook hands when he walked in, and he gave his first name to the hostess. I still didn't know his last name at this point and hadn't been able to Google him—which I hated. But our conversation that night flowed perfectly. I can't tell you another time I've ever been able to just hang out with a guy and talk and talk and talk. Our conversation was so easy, and after we'd been there for *two and a half hours*, I still wasn't ready to go. He hadn't asked me a single question about Jeff or even the kids. Our whole date was just about getting to know each other. I didn't even notice that at first, but it was so refreshing. He later told me it was because his best friends were in the midst of a divorce and he knew it was a sensitive topic.

When it was finally time to make our way home, he walked me to my car, and we had a casual hug goodnight. We talked about trying to go out again that weekend.

When I pulled in the driveway, I texted him to thank him for a great night and that I was looking forward to seeing him again. Josh and I to this day still read that text differently. I was merely being polite, and he claims I was clearly so into him that I couldn't even wait until he was home to start texting him.

But actually, I knew when I walked in the door to relieve my mom from babysitting, I'd get sidetracked and never follow up. And I try really hard to be polite.

When I walked in the house, I collapsed on the couch, and my mom asked, "So how was it?"

"I don't really know. I mean, we stayed at dinner talking for over two hours, but I have no idea if I actually liked him or not."

On our second date, four days later, we spent almost six hours together going to different breweries downtown, and we ended the evening with one chaste kiss. I'd ambushed him that morning and told him I'd meet him at his house so we could ride together and then he didn't have to know where I lived yet... but I just wanted to be able to see his place and get a better sense of who this guy was.

He told me he spent all morning cleaning and that he'd only finished minutes before I got there, and he was still sweating from it!

After two dates with him, I came back to this question I had the previous fall.

How does The Bachelorette do it?

Those men and women make it look so easy to kiss, hug, and generally get all lovey-dovey. But what I found is that I can't just meet someone for the first time and suddenly be ready to go there. In fact, the whole idea of doing anything more than kiss absolutely terrified me! I'd been with Jeff since I was twenty, and he's all I'd ever really known. And being twenty and innocent somehow made it all so much easier.

Now, I had all of this life experience that I brought to the table, but I didn't have any dating experience! And I was baffled. I didn't know how to behave.

Date #3 was really pivotal to me. He came over after I had the kids in bed, a technique we used for a while, so I wasn't relying on my parents so much for babysitting. Neither one of us was making a move as we hung out awkwardly on the couch watching something on tv. Then standing in the kitchen we finally had more than a casual kiss. A night of hot and heavy making out was all it took. It made me realize how sex really could confuse your emotions and make you feel things that aren't real. I was feeling them even with a drawn out make out session.

But regardless of whether those feelings were real or not, Josh was such a good guy and I was having a great time with him. So, I continued following the advice of my girlfriends to "stay out of my head."

This is just dating.

I am allowed to just have fun. So that's what I did. But I did it my way—which is responsibly. I made him get tested for STIs, and I waited until I knew we were exclusive before I did anything I was afraid I'd regret later. I didn't introduce him to the kids as my boyfriend until I knew it was serious.

After about a month of dating, I took the kids on a trip to visit their cousins, and Josh missed me a lot.

"I miss having you around," he texted.

"Can you send me a picture?" he asked.

I was hanging out in the living room at the time, while Ryan played with a remote-controlled car, and asked him to pause and take the picture. I sat casually on the bottom of the stairs in a flannel shirt.

To this day, Josh tells me it's one of his favorite pictures of me.

Honestly, I couldn't decide if I missed him or not. I did miss being around him, but I felt fine being away too. Was that just because I was the one on vacation and busy? I wasn't sure! My life was so full that I wasn't sure I had room in my heart for more.

Josh was so accommodating though, and he made me realize what a big deal it is for a man to date a single parent like me. Most of our "dates" were him coming over after bedtime and staying for two hours to talk, watch tv, and have a make out session.

I know I was supposed to be staying out of my head and having fun, but I just didn't want to hold on too long only to break his heart. What if he was sitting there thinking he could marry me?

After about six weeks of dating, Josh invited me to Key West with him. I thought he was crazy, but I'd also never been—and he was paying. I don't know why, but I decided it could be a fun weekend away and would be a great way to figure out my feelings and see him in his element with friends.

Between the time I said yes to the trip and when it was time to go, we made a lot of progress in our relationship. He met the kids and started hanging out with us some.

Even though we kept all PDA non-existent, Peyton was no dummy. She got attached really fast. So much so that I had to pump the breaks on all of his interactions with her. She begged for him to put her to bed whenever he was over in the evenings.

One night when she'd weaseled her way into a bedtime routine with Josh, he tucked her in and she pulled him close whispering, "Sing me a song."

"I don't know any songs," he told her.

"Well you know your ABCs. Sing me that."

And there was no arguing that! He did know his ABCs.

I listened and watched the baby monitor with the biggest grin on my face as it all went down.

When Peyton's closet light went out a week later, the entire fixture had to be replaced, and Josh offered to come do it for me!

And he actually did it.

I was blown away. I purposely tried not to rely on him for any household thing like that, but I wasn't going to turn him down either. Otherwise, I would have been paying for an electrician.

A week before Key West, I met one of his friends at dinner, and she was great. I wasn't sure what to expect, but I really liked her. She told me (while Josh was in the bathroom) that she'd asked him if he had told me he loved me yet.

Yikes. I knew he was falling, but I was still caught off guard when she said that. But I'm so glad she did. It gave me time to prepare since it was probably coming out in Key West.

Our flight was so peaceful going down. What a change to travel with someone not afraid of flying. I rested on his shoulder, and we read books and listened to our music. I could feel my shoulders lightening.

We picked up our rental car, and as we were settling in for our romantic long weekend, the check engine light came on. He was flooring it and we were barely able to go 60 mph. Something was definitely wrong. Ugh, and my mom had made me promise that I'd come back alive.

Eventually, Josh pulled off at an exit while I was on the phone with the roadside assistance people. How was there no rental place we could stop and swap out our car?! Finally, they located an extra car, and we drove carefully to a nearby branch to swap them out.

Josh was outwardly super calm, and I couldn't believe how well he kept his cool. We were sitting in a random Advanced Auto parking lot unsure of if or when we'd be able to get a replacement vehicle, and he showed no sign of ruffled feathers—even though when I ask him about that today, he said he was totally frustrated. But in the moment, I felt like he passed a big relationship test!

After we swapped out cars, we made it down Route 1 for a sunset dinner and drinks at our hotel for the night while we waited for his friends to arrive. Once we were settled, we sat outside in a lounge chair by the pool, empty and all lit up and peaceful. We were just enjoying the time alone and getting to know each other more. Then, while I'm leaning against him in the lounge chair, I feel his deep breath inhale.

"You got me," he said—implying he was falling for me. No 'I love you' explosions yet.

But the very next morning, without any warning, he busts out with, "I think I'm falling in love with you."

Even though I knew it was coming, I still couldn't give a proper response. I was so disappointed in myself. After all that practice, I couldn't do better than a thank you! I hid in his chest with a smile and eventually said thank you—and I was glad to hear him say that, but that I wasn't there yet.

He said, "I knew it last week when we were watching *Guardians of the Galaxy* and I knew that I didn't want to be anywhere else."

(*For the record, that may be the most romantic thing he's ever spoken to me.*)

I wasn't even able to talk to him more about it until we were in the airport on the way home. I just didn't know how to express how I felt and why I wasn't *there*. I'm not even completely sure why I wasn't there. He was really in to me, and it made me nervous. Jeff was the same, and it didn't matter.

I told Josh that I was definitely falling for him, but it was just so hard for me to let my guard down and fully trust him. Jeff loved me more than anything, and in the end, he still chose alcohol over me, and over our kids.

What I didn't share was how much the idea of a future with him terrified me. Like, I could *see* a life with him. And that completely and totally freaked me out. I was resigned that I'd be single forever, and it was so hard to think I found someone who could be forever.

And yet, there I sat, post-trip—still confused. I sat there thinking in my head every time we would text that I wanted to say 'I love you' and I didn't know why.

He was so good to me and such a solid guy. I liked so much about him, and I hated that I could picture a future with him so quickly. I told him about what a hard time Peyton was having with her male coaches recently, and he asked if it would help if he went with us to practice to encourage her. I mean, REALLY. What a gem, as my friend Katie would say. And for the first time, I could really say that I missed him!

Our summer continued to build on this foundation. I had Jeff's cousin's family stay with me one weekend, and although I hadn't originally planned on Josh spending much time with us, he was over every day. And he loved them, and they loved him. It could have been awkward or something he wanted to stay away from, but instead, he leaned in fully—manning the grill and making us dinner one night. After Jeff left, that grill had basically gone unused for two years. When Josh went to cook, it wasn't even in working condition. He deep cleaned it, got it started, and then cooked all the food! It was amazing. Things like that are what made me melt for him.

Josh had also started to discipline the kids more. Usually, I felt good about that, but other times it bothered me. It made me feel like he thought they weren't well-behaved. And yes, they are a handful, and weren't the best-behaved, but with all they'd been through, it was so hard knowing how to deal with them and what level of discipline to give.

A week later, we were all in the car together and Peyton said, "Josh looks like someone who is moving in."

We laughed and asked her what she meant.

She said, "Well he's always at our house."

Such an observant little thing. She also asked Josh if he was going to be her new daddy.

And he said, "I don't know."

Back up. *I don't know?!*

So was he thinking about forever? I mean, I was, but was he too?!

Chapter 21

Falling in love again

As the summer went on, I found myself thinking about Josh more and wanting to be around him. I found comfort in him, and I let him do more things for me that I should be independent enough to be doing myself. But the security of him felt good. I felt protected, safe and happy with him.

He met a bunch of my friends at a wedding. That was a great night. How wonderful to go to an event and not be embarrassed by my date! We stuck together a lot, but I also spent a ton of time on the dance floor with the girls while he sat back with the guys and talked. He went out in the pouring rain, at the end of the night, to get the car and bring back an umbrella for me and my friend. He was solid.

He was there for Ryan's birthday party, which was all family plus him and my friend Katie. He manned the grill and was the very last person to leave that day. He hung out with my family, and even went to Party City to get me crazy oversized Avengers balloons for the party!

I started telling him 'I love you' a bit more often. We still didn't say it a ton, but I think it was right. We both jumped the gun initially, but my feelings continued to grow stronger for him. The first time I spit it out was after he put together a new bed for Ryan. I got caught up in the moment, feeling thankful for such a tedious gesture.

We spent all of July 4th weekend together and had a blast. We went to another wedding, and he and I had a lot of alone time to wander at the reception and talk. It was just peaceful and happy.

The next night we went out to a farm for a cookout and big fireworks show, and Josh helped set them off. He thought he was just going to set up and be polite, and then when he got to light those monsters, he was pretty stoked and pleased with himself! The kids and I sat in the back of his truck and watched, and it just felt like family.

The last day of the holiday weekend, we went car shopping. It was the one big purchase I wanted to make with my insurance money since the kids and I are on the go so much. At this point, Josh had no clue I had this nest egg for the kids. I told him I'd just saved my car payment amount each month for the last few years since I'd paid off my car. It's the type of responsible thing I'd do anyway.

Josh was so attentive and patient and smart. He wanted to make sure I wasn't settling on something I didn't really want just because of the price and he did so much research during the week to help make sure I got it.

As we drove around that day, we spent some time talking about Jeff's downfall. I think hearing the story meant more to him now that he knew me and the kids more. He couldn't believe that Jeff hadn't seen the kids for six months before he died. It's hard for anyone to comprehend that.

I was still afraid thinking about our future. I tried to stay lucid and focused on my head and not let my fantasy of a happy little life distract me, but it was hard. I pictured my life with Josh and knew what a great partner he'd be, so sometimes I'd wonder if I was in the right headspace and wasn't being critical enough. But thinking about forever made me simultaneously so happy and so terrified. The fear of the unknown, of making a mistake—it paralyzed me.

That week was the pinnacle of seeing how special Josh is and how much he cared about me. We'd been waiting and waiting on my car deal to come through, and Josh kept doing research and looking at more options. Despite working late nights, he was willing to leave early and drive two hours with me to pick up a car. Then before we made the decision to drive, he told me I should call my local guy one more time to give him a chance to match the offer. It felt like unnecessary effort since he never called me back the day before, but I did. After some hard negotiating, I got the price I wanted, and all I sacrificed were some all-weather mats and the cross rails.

It was awesome, and I felt so grateful to Josh for all his help. So that weekend we went out to dinner to celebrate, my treat! I was officially crazy about him.

———————————◆———————————

At the end of the month, I'd invited Josh to join me, the kids, and my parents for part of our annual beach trip to North Carolina. I felt like leaving early in the morning for the beach was a good excuse for Josh to have a sleepover while the kids were in the house.

I asked Peyton if that was okay and where she thought he should sleep.

"He could sleep in my room," she said.

"Peyton, I think your bed is too small for him."

She noodled on that for a second and then said, "Well, your bed is really big. He could sleep in your room."

So, that's what we did.

We packed up the car and Peyton and I rode down in Josh's truck, while my mom took Ryan in my car. It was a really fun day. We stopped in Wilmington and I made Josh take our picture at "Peyton's house" from *One Tree Hill,* her namesake, then we went to the waterfront for lunch and bought a few souvenirs before finishing the drive to the beach.

Josh only stayed for three days before he had to go back for work, and the whole time he was there, I couldn't help but feel like he was distant and not super into me.

All I could think was, if he wants to break up, just do it. I'd been through so much worse and would be fine. Don't drag it out—for everyone's sake. It was a reminder to me that if he wasn't the one, then he was the one who was supposed to show me how good love can be and what kind of man I deserved.

If Josh and I didn't work out, then I hoped Peyton could move on without a lot of hurt. She asked if Josh could be her new daddy and talked about us getting married all the time, with NO prompting or encouraging from me. It was embarrassing, but Josh said that I was more uncomfortable about it than he was. So, at least, he wasn't running for the hills.

If it did turn out to be Josh, I can't even comprehend the blessings God has given me. I prayed and prayed to find someone quickly so the kids would have a dad and be raised by him. I didn't want their stepdad to only know them when they were older. I wanted him to know them their whole lives, or as close to it as possible. And Josh being here since Ryan was two and a half is pretty special.

———————————— ◆ ————————————

Alas, we didn't break up. He didn't realize he'd been acting differently at the beach and making me nervous about our relationship. I tried to stuff down those fears of losing him and what it would do to the kids.

It had been six unbelievable months with Josh. I was learning so much about myself and the things I needed in a relationship. I was shocked with how insecure I could suddenly feel in his feelings for me. When I think about *The 5 Love Languages* by Gary Chapman (a must-read if you're unfamiliar), I now understand that I wholly rely on words of affirmation to make me feel confident in his feelings for me. I just couldn't wrap my head around him being fully okay with me and the kids as a package deal, and I kept waiting for that *one thing* to happen that pushed him too far and he realized that he couldn't do it.

I look at what he does for me and how he treats me and makes me feel, and I just had no idea it could be this way. I was so smitten and felt so happy and safe and protected. Josh is someone who was made to be a provider and he would make such a good partner in this crazy life. Everything with him just felt so simple. Like, *is this how easy it should be??* People talk about marriage being such hard work, and I know it is, but I wondered how the workload felt when you had a partner like him.

I asked him if he'd thought about introducing the kids to his family, and he said he hadn't really thought about it. He said maybe Christmas. Which felt SO. FAR. AWAY. I just needed to feel like everyone was on board with me and with them, and I won't be judged or considered a disappointment that I'm bringing them into everyone's life.

Bottom line, I was in. I loved him, and I was having a hard time not picturing life with him now. I wanted to fast forward six months and make it to a year together. I wanted to make it a lot longer than that. Like, forever.

Chapter 22

Risking it all

I read something once about dating as a single parent: *How much are you willing to risk breaking your child all over again?*

That was the general sentiment. It's such a fine line, right? I want and deserve love, and someone deserves my love. And my kids deserve the best mom I can be. And they deserve a happy life with just enough struggle to keep them grounded. Divorce has been shown over and over to have painful impacts on kids, and a parent's death? I'm sure that causes trauma in its own right.

But sometimes I really can't believe how blessed I am. In fact, I often struggle with it because it doesn't seem fair that I got complete closure with Jeff and everything I prayed for appeared to be coming true. I asked for a man to love me with kindness and be a dad to the kids. Someone who could be in their lives since they were little. A person who the kids can't recall NOT being in their lives. Could it really be this simple for me? If Josh is the one for me, then it would be.

And yet, I was terrified of my relationship with Josh. Terrified that it wouldn't work out, and I'd break their hearts again. I knew I wouldn't do this again. This dating thing. It's too much work and too easy to break them. If it wasn't going to be him, it just couldn't be anyone but me and the kids.

Then I was terrified that I'd accidentally force my relationship with Josh because I wanted it to work out so badly. I was afraid something would happen that should have been my signal to leave, and I'd miss it because I wanted it to work.

But I thought about all of the amazing times I'd had with him so far, and I saw how I should be treated. I saw how a relationship should be and should feel, and it really breaks my heart at how mistreated I was with Jeff. I knew—but I didn't know. We didn't have a good relationship, and I really started to struggle with the memories of our marriage. Every happy memory I recall, I remember something bad that happened after. It's hard. It's also good. It makes me appreciate Josh and what a relationship can and should be.

I remember talking to my sister-in-law when she got engaged, and she talked about this ring she loved from Sam's Club that was $500. All I remember thinking *for years* was how weird that was.

Why? This is YOUR RING. That you'll wear every day for the rest of your life, hopefully!

They had a really nice wedding, but she never seemed too concerned with the dress, the showers, or anything that I really recall. At the time, I chalked it up to her being a medical resident and not having the time to plan a big wedding.

Now, I totally get her. It's hard to believe she was married to someone before Chris. While they don't seem like a 'perfect' couple by any means (whatever that is!), they fit. And they respect each other. And they work hard on their marriage. I've come to admire them so much as time has gone on.

When I'd go to Costco, I enter and walk right by the jewelry without a glance. And now, I stop sometimes and look at the bling over there. And then I look at the price and see that I love some ring that is only $1500. And suddenly, I get her view. The price doesn't matter. Pick something you love. Don't spend a fortune. The man matters, not the ring.

And when I'd think about a wedding, I really couldn't care less. The only part that mattered to me was getting married in the church that saved me and healed me. Being married in a place of God and doing the proper counseling prior to marriage. These are what mattered to me, and after that, it's whatever is important to him. I didn't want the showers and didn't want the spectacle. I wanted the good man and the good marriage.

Peyton was in first grade by this point. She was doing some family project and had to bring in a photo. She told the teacher, "I don't have a dad anymore, but I'm getting a new one soon."

Lord, help me. Not only was I so embarrassed when her teacher told me this, but how did I help her understand reality? We were seriously dating at this point, but that didn't make him her soon-to-be dad. Did I hope it worked out like she described and expected? Of course! But then the fear—how hard will it be for us if that's not the case? The kids talked about Josh all the time. Would it hurt them? Have I kept him enough on our periphery that it would be okay if things didn't work out?

A few weeks later, we went to the pumpkin patch together. We picked out pumpkins then spent a long time playing on the swings and seesaw. Josh did such a great job playing with the kids, and when Peyton was climbing up the slide ladder, she just casually said to him, "I love you Josh."

heart melts

And he replied, "I love you too."

Then she asked us to kiss in front of everyone, and Josh told Peyton to come closer, and he kissed her on *her* cheek instead.

She did not like it. And a few minutes later, she pulled me aside to whisper, "I did not like it when Josh kissed me. I do not forgive him."

Well, color me confused. I didn't understand it, but of course, I told her that was okay, and he didn't have to kiss her if she didn't want him to. It was an odd reaction, but it was the first of many times she'd flip-flop on her feelings about Josh.

We ended that day with dinner at my parents' house, and Josh played outside with me and the kids after we ate. We were all wiped, but it was a great day. I went to bed that night feeling so lucky and loved.

———————◆———————

At Christmas time, Josh, Peyton, and I went to The Nutcracker with some friends. After the show, we were walking back to our car in the garage, and Josh asked Peyton to give him a hug. She hid behind me for a bit but eventually collapsed into him. He told her he loved her and also loved Mommy.

When Peyton and I were alone, we had a long conversation about why Josh and I weren't engaged. She couldn't understand how I could be in love with him but then not want to marry him. It was very black and white. I tried to explain that marriage is a big decision and we can't rush. And how important it was to me that she and Ryan love Josh.

And she replied, "But I DO love Josh. I want him to be my dad."

———————◆———————

I had done my best to stay in touch with Jeff's parents, but the reality was we only saw them a few times a year. They weren't comfortable coming to meet us at the house Jeff and I shared, which I understood, so our visits were usually at Chick-fil-a.

When we arrived for our Christmas visit, Opa (what the kids called Jeff's dad) called himself Santa since he had presents waiting for them.

"But you don't have a beard," Peyton said.

"Josh has a beard," Ryan said.

"Mommy kisses Josh," Peyton said.

OMG. Just let me curl up in a ball and hide right now! I'd been debating how to approach the topic of Josh, but I couldn't find the guts on how to bring it up. They were aware of him, but we didn't exactly talk about him and the seriousness of our relationship.

Our visit went really well despite my embarrassment. The kids opened their presents and we had lunch together then played in the play area. And after successfully making it through that visit, I was able to relax and enjoy the rest of the holiday break.

Christmas was so magical that year. It was such a happy, family occasion. Peyton was in the Nativity play at church for the first time, and it was so fun seeing her up there and reciting her words! She memorized it so much faster than I imagined, and she wasn't even as nervous as I expected. My parents and Josh's family came to church with us, and then we all went back to my house for dinner after. Things were so easy, and it all appeared to go smoothly.

Josh's mom seemed to accept us. She wanted to get the kids a present, so they'd have something to open when we went to their house on Christmas day. It was so nice, and his family was so gracious to us. I prayed that it was sincere and not just polite. This family seemed like they could make good in-laws down the road.

Chapter 23

Crazy girl

We moved into the new year with a sermon series at church that coincidentally focused on marriage. The first day of it was during a snowstorm, so Josh and I bundled up on the couch and watched a livestream of worship. I adored sitting and snuggling with him while we listened to this great message— putting God first and your spouse second, then your kids, and then your work.

"I've been putting work first," he said. "I want to work on that."

It was true that for Josh, who had never been in a long-term relationship like this, work was his main priority in life. Sometimes he'd work until 2AM, and I'd remind him how crazy that was— and how unreasonable it was for someone with a family.

There was a daily bible plan that went along with the series, so I participated in that all month long. One part focused on praying for your partner, so I worked hard to pray for Josh in various parts of his life—focus at work, discipline over food, and putting more focus on me and the kids.

To this day, praying for Josh is something that I put high on my priority list. If we're struggling with something or if he's having an issue, sometimes I'll literally walk around our bed or lay on his side and pray for him and for us. Literally circling him in prayer over and over with the same prayer for a month, or longer.

We were coming up on our first year together, and it was time to celebrate Valentine's Day for the first time. Jeff's birthday was around Valentine's Day, so it was never really a holiday that he and I celebrated. It was always a celebration of him, which I never had a problem with. Valentine's Day had never been a holiday that mattered to me much.

So, I downplayed the day and told Josh that all I wanted was a nice card and chocolate covered cherries, my favorite holiday treat. And I realized that when I got exactly that (and only that!), well, it turns out I actually did care about Valentine's Day. Up to this point, he'd always been so on point with holidays or surprises, so I kept expecting my phone to ring to go pick up flowers from the front desk. Or at least to have them waiting for me when I got home. Or *something* in addition to buying exactly what I told him to buy me. Lesson learned. Spell out what I want and be honest. Don't downplay.

I'd been super crafty and had his office manager leave a card on his desk to surprise him when he came in, and I all but said 'I'd marry you tomorrow' in it. I poured my heart out to him, and I thought this was a good opportunity for him to reciprocate that sentiment. I'd asked not just for a card, but for him to *write me* something sweet in the card. And he did. Short and sweet. He said he hoped he'd have years of Valentine's Day cards to give me. In boy words, I think that's a pretty solid declaration.

Without prompting that evening, he acknowledged the depth of the card I gave him and apologized for not being as verbose. But I needed him to follow that with, "But I feel that way about you too" or something of the same effect. I wished I didn't feel so insecure, but I was always on edge waiting for the other shoe to drop. It was too hard to fathom that my life could turn out this happy and easy.

As we finished the marriage series at church, I started reading *The Power of the Praying Wife.* It's such a different way to look at marriage and your partnership, and although I considered myself a progressive, 21st century girl, I also really love the idea of having a safe and secure marriage filed with respect and love. I love praying not only for Josh but for me to change my feelings and my heart so that certain things about him do not bother me, which is one of the themes in the book.

Despite this sermon series and all this talk about praying for Josh, I noticed myself unable to connect with him when we went to Florida for our first anniversary together. We had a great time, and nothing went wrong, but I kept having these CRAZY

GIRL feelings like something was wrong. You know that feeling? Where suddenly you're looking for a hidden meaning in every meaningless action and convinced doom is inevitable? I was totally sure nothing was actually wrong, but I still couldn't shake it off.

First, I noticed that I was picking at him the way I used to pick on Jeff. The biggest thing that I promised myself I'd work on with this relationship was to be positive and encouraging. I don't think there's anything healthy or positive about teasing your partner in front of others, and I kept finding myself doing it that weekend we were with his friends.

"Oh, look at your shirt, it's a mess."

"Geez, take a breath while you eat. Chew with your mouth closed."

Maybe it was just because it was Josh's friends and they would rag on each other and it rubbed off on me, but maybe it was something else.

I noticed several times that weekend that other couples were walking and holding hands, and we weren't. It made me self-conscious.

A year earlier in Key West, it was okay that we weren't holding hands like everyone else. We were new. No "I Love You" yet. But now, we were talking marriage. I wanted to be in love and intimate with him. I wanted to be in close, physical contact with him all the time. It was then I realized that his random moments of making me feel loved had disappeared. Which, don't get me wrong, he still made me feel so loved (which is why I say I had CRAZY GIRL thoughts). The problem was, those moments just weren't as frequent now.

When we got back from our trip, I kept making myself work up the nerve to tell him about the crazy feelings I'd been having. I prayed for the strength to talk to him about this, and I kept chickening out. I rehearsed it in my head a dozen times. But I still couldn't muster the strength to talk him. And that worried me on a few levels. First, it was important that we could discuss important things. Sometimes I felt like we were too surface level. Second, it was important that I felt comfortable telling him when something bothered me. And look how silly I was acting? I kept putting off the conversation.

Sometimes in my 'devil on my shoulder' moments, I wondered if I was supposed to be with him. I wondered if things were unraveling, and these were my signs. I wondered if the best moments had passed or if I was holding on for the kids and our happy ending... or, HELLO. Shut up. You are CRAZY and letting the devil try and steal your happiness.

I truly can't believe the gift God gave me by putting Josh in my path, by not letting me give up on him or the idea of giving my time to him. I can't comprehend the blessings bestowed on me. It's a lot of pressure to live up to sometimes.

And yet, as I sat watching The Bachelor finale (Nick's season!), Vanessa questioned if love was enough. If Nick felt "a bit more" for her than he did for Raven (*did you even remember that they were his final two?*), could that really be enough for her? It made me lonely for some reason.

I was two seconds from calling Josh and asking him to come spend the night with me. I didn't know what is wrong with me, but even after I told Josh about my crazy girl feelings and he promised to work on it, I still felt it. I had so much pain in my heart wondering how to deal with my emotions. I felt such a pull to him when he'd leave at the end of the night or when he wasn't here, and I struggled so hard with what that meant. Was I so stuck in infatuation and wanting a happy ending? Or did I truly love this man and want to spend my life with him? Was that pull towards him something higher, more spiritual and meaningful?

———————————— ◆ ————————————

Josh's birthday was a month later. He spent the night so that we could all wake up in the morning and do our family birthday traditions for him—balloons and cupcakes to kick off the day. The kids woke us up early, and I left Josh in bed while we went downstairs to decorate cupcakes, blow up balloons, and put up streamers.

He left us after breakfast so he could run some errands, and he took his god-daughter with him, who is about Ryan's age, and he came home telling me how great the trip was with her.

When we started dating, I thought it was so weird that Josh's (female) good friend told him she was nervous I'd be jealous of her. It never crossed my mind that would be the case. What also never dawned on me was that I'd be jealous of her kids though. He adores them. From the beginning, I thought they were one of the greatest benefits as to why we'd worked out. He could accept my kids because he'd been so close to another set of kids around the same age.

But now, while I could tell he accepted and loved my kids, they weren't his number one yet. At least, I didn't feel that way. Adjusting to this "relationship" life was tough for him, I could tell. He was struggling with how to split his time with me, my kids, and them—and still have Josh time.

"I need to plan out my calendar better so I can make sure I spend more time with everyone," he'd say.

I so desperately wanted to believe he cared about my kids the way he cared about his Godchildren. I needed MY babies to be his babies. I needed him to love them as if they were his children. If we got married, he was going to *be* their dad. And no dad should want other children more than his own.

I couldn't make sense of my feelings and why I was struggling with insecurity again. Did I just think the happily ever after wasn't going to happen? Did I think he didn't want it to? Did I not want it to? *What* was wrong with me?

I just knew I was going to explode if I didn't share with him how I was feeling, and I knew he'd hate to know I went to bed crying over my uncertainty. I had no idea how to broach it with him, so I started by saying, "I feel like I could marry you tomorrow… and that really freaks me out."

I continued, "You are so important to me, but I need to know that you can love Peyton and Ryan the way I do—that you feel like their dad and they come first for you — or rather, like we heard in the marriage sermon series—God first, spouse second, kids third, then work. That's the order I'm looking for from you. Not your Godchildren before my kids."

He acknowledged the struggle to balance everyone's emotions but promised to keep trying. "I'm not quite ready to marry you tomorrow, but I'm getting there," he said.

I knew he meant it to be positive, and maybe to throw me off his scent that he was actually going to be ring shopping a couple of weeks later, but ouch. I left our conversation thinking maybe a ring wasn't coming as soon as I thought.

———————◆———————

Nine days after that conversation, things were feeling really good. Josh and his mom came to watch Peyton at swim champs, and his mom was *recording the races on her phone*! My heart was in all kinds of happy knots.

That night, we dropped the kids off with his mom for a sleepover. She had been offering to babysit and keep them overnight, so I took her up on it to give my parents a weekend off. The kids had been looking forward to it so much, especially Peyton. I was a nervous wreck about it though—will his mom get tired? Will the kids behave? Will someone wet the bed? Or get up at 2AM? So much could go wrong.

Thankfully the kids were good, even though Ryan did get up at 5AM! She made them pancakes and did an Easter Egg hunt throughout the house. I saw her without make up for the first time, so I know they kept her busy!

But she was so nice about it all and even sent an email thanking me for letting her keep them and saying what a nice job I'd done raising them. It was so sweet and so important to me for my future with Josh.

During our night off, Josh and I had dinner out and went to a concert. We got there early and hung out with a drink and just talked. He asked me if I'd started saving for college, and how he knew one day he'd realize just how expensive kids were. He still didn't know about my life insurance money at this point, but I knew he was on board regardless of what I brought to the table. I wanted to tell him, but I kept holding off not knowing if he was truly committed to me.

———————◆———————

After that night, he came down with something and I didn't see him for several days. It had been about four days since our date night, and he texted me, "I totally miss you by the way."

That was all I needed. I don't ask for a lot, but reassurance and verbalized feelings like that—that's it. That's what fills my love tank. He melted my heart for the first time in forever—I really can't remember the last time he made me feel that happy—Christmas, maybe? That seems silly, but it really reinforced how words of affirmation had become such a dominant love language for me post-Jeff.

I responded with, "🖤 nicest thing you've said in a while ;) thank you! I totally miss you too."

The next night, Josh told me I'd upset him with that response. He didn't take it like I was being snarky, but worse, sincere—and it made him want to try and be more vocal to meet my needs. He randomly followed up with, "The only reason I said I wasn't quite ready to marry you tomorrow is because I think people would be pretty pissed off if we didn't invite them to a wedding."

I thought it was funny that he knew I had probably been stewing on that comment and dissecting what it meant.

Chapter 24

Forever and ever

Spring was nearly perfect that year. Josh and I were inseparable and so happy, and I was about to transition to a new role at work. Things were exciting and the future looked so bright.

But then a hiring freeze and reorganization happened at work, and the new role I was supposed to have was no longer available to me. I had to stay put. And worse, I'd lost my direct manager who had been such a great advocate for me.

My department head wanted to talk to me about staying under her with this restructure, but I was a HOT MESS. Any time I thought about what transpired, I cried. And I didn't want to talk to her and be sobbing. She and I had about three conversations in the three and a half years I'd worked for her, and she didn't deserve to see my tears.

I cried some more when I walked out of the building that day, and then I started putting it all back into perspective. I had a job. I had a job I already knew how to do really well. I could coast through until something else came up. I didn't like the VP option, and I hated the manager shake up, but I could do this job easily. And I could do it with minimum effort and get by.

I reminded myself how unimportant this outcome was after all the shit that I'd dealt with over the last three years. And while I was still super disappointed, I felt like that revelation really spoke to my growth and ability to recognize pain and prioritize how much energy to give it.

It disappoints me that I still struggled with waves of PTSD over the previous few years because I considered myself so strong. And so, when someone didn't view me as this awesome person who overcame a shit ton of crazy, it bothered me. And that's how I felt about this department head I worked for. I never had any validation from her, about my ability to maintain high quality work during that time. AND I'M JUST SO DAMN PROUD OF HOW I DID IT ALL. I wasn't expecting to take work so personally.

It's just another example of how I needed to stop expecting from others. How I feel about myself and what I believe needed to be enough, and at the end of the day, I needed to look inward to really feel satisfied with myself and my situation. I'm no expert at this by any means, but when I do find myself getting upset about how others view me, I stay upset for less time, and the pain it causes is less intense.

It only took me about three more months to finally get out from under her, but I'm still working on regaining my confidence at work two years later. Thankfully I moved to a team that supported my development and also outwardly expressed how impressed they were with my composure and ability to produce quality work during such a challenging personal time.

The challenging personal times were starting to feel like they were behind me.

———◆———

Josh gave me a ring.

We'd been out for an event of Ryan's, and my mom took him home with her after so Josh and I could go to dinner. His mom had Peyton for the night.

We went to Bonefish, where we had our first date. I don't think there was any significance to planning it that way. We just really like the Bang Bang Shrimp, and I think we had a gift card!

When we got home, I was in the bathroom removing my makeup, and he busts in with a red ring box. I literally cannot recall a thing he said, and I so wanted to give him a hard time for the lack of lovey-dovey words for me, but I'm sure he was both so excited and nervous and I didn't want to be rude. I'm not sure there was an actual question or proposal in there, but whatever he said was a blur.

The ring was beautiful, and he told me he'd planned to propose at the beach a few months later but when the ring came in this past Monday, he just knew he'd never make it that long. After he'd accepted a new job that week and been so stressed about it, he said *this* decision wasn't hard at all and he figured, "Why not make it a big week?"

The next morning, Josh wanted to buy Peyton her own special piece of jewelry so I wouldn't be the only one with something sparkly. I gave a couple of suggestions, but I left it to him to pick the piece. He chose a simple heart filled with little diamonds. It was so sweet of him to do that for her. Not to be left out (but not knowing what to get a 3-year-old boy!), we got Ryan a Disney toy and a mini Gravedigger monster truck.

When we all got back to the house, Josh told Peyton we had a surprise for her. Her first guess in the car had been getting to do gymnastics classes, and her second guess was that we were getting married.

When we confirmed her second guess and I flashed her my ring, she showed the most sincere joy I've ever seen in my life. She screamed and immediately ran into Josh's arms and said, "I LOVE YOU!"

It was the first time I cried over the engagement. So terribly sweet and beautiful. Within an hour, she was asking me if he was moving in, when we were getting married, can she call him Dad...

I called Jeff's brother that afternoon, and he seemed happy for us.

"I've been waiting for this call," he said. "I think Josh is the right one for you."

It was pretty funny timing because I'd just finished reading *Option B* by Sheryl Sandberg, and I had mailed it to both Chris and his mom. His mom started reading hers immediately, and there's a large section in there about moving on after a spouse dies and finding someone new.

Chris told me his mom seemed genuinely happy for us when he told her the news. I hope that was a little thanks to the book and it really does help her heal.

We had a busy first month post-engagement. We picked a date only six months away, decided to build a house, and Josh was prepping to move in. It was all a bit of a whirlwind, so I guess it was for the best that I didn't also start a new job during all of this. God's timing works in funny ways.

Now that Josh was getting more comfortable parenting the kids, we were facing some new challenges. Peyton got upset with Josh when he would discipline Ryan, and when he would discipline her. She called him "rude" whenever he yelled at them or got mad. We kept correcting her that it's called parenting and teaching them the right way to behave, and that it's because she or Ryan was acting rude, not us.

In bed one night, she and I were snuggling and she said, "I want to tell you something but you'll get mad."

"It's okay. You can tell me, even if you think it will upset me."

"I hate Josh. I don't want you to get married," she complained.

When I probed, it was once again because he was "so rude" when he yelled at Ryan. I so naively thought she was young enough that she'd completely welcome Josh as her dad and be thrilled to have him, but when it came to discipline, the first thing she'd say is that she wished she had her daddy here, not Josh.

I explained that if her dad was here, he would discipline her the same way Josh did. She and Ryan would get in trouble when they didn't behave. He'd yell at them, spank them. All of it. Since her daddy couldn't be here, I reminded her how lucky she was to have Josh with us to love us and care about us.

This feeling of hers didn't go away.

We went to the beach at the end of the summer with my parents and my friend and her son. I'd just finished this amazing parenting book called *How to Talk So Kids Will Listen and Listen So Kids Will Talk*, and I'd been trying to put its theories into use. Josh hadn't read it yet and wasn't convinced that it was doing any good and that their behavior was actually getting worse.

Ryan had recently started a new phase of stomping and screaming when he got frustrated, so he had been a challenge at home and at school. One night early in the week, Ryan did some back-talking after dinner and Josh yanked him up out of the room and told him Nonnie wasn't putting him to bed, which is what they loved when she was around.

Well, you know that look of terror on a kid's face when they think something really bad is about to happen—like getting spanked or punished in some way? Ryan's face had that look of terror on him as he screamed and cried. It just about broke my heart, and I know my mom *hated* it.

I went back in his room with them to help calm him since I couldn't bear that look either, and Ryan calmed himself pretty quickly. He didn't want Josh to put him down, so Josh just sat on the bed while I laid with Ryan and read him some stories and snuggled with him until he fell asleep.

When we came back out, my mom seemed upset. I asked her if she was mad at me, and she got emotional and just said, "I can't talk about it."

Then she walked outside and sat on the porch with my dad—which eliminated him as the guilty party.

I wasn't sure what I'd done, but I assumed that meant she was mad at me. I decided to go out there and ask what was wrong.

She started crying. "I don't like the way Josh treats the kids. He is too hard on them, and I'm worried about all of this."

My dad, who never says anything, chimed in, "He needs to learn to cut them some slack."

"We just can't go through this again," she said. "And it's all happening so fast."

"We just want to make sure you're not making a mistake or feeling controlled or pressured into marrying Josh," she continued.

I was so taken aback by their comments, and it shook me hard. I assured them that was not the case.

"Yes, he is tough sometimes, but they also need more discipline in their lives. They've spent the last three years with me just getting by," I tried to explain.

Yes, he was strict with the kids and gave them tough love, but he was also learning to be a parent for the first time. Instead of getting to be there from the beginning so he could learn with each stage, he got thrown into the mix with two rambunctious and not exactly the most well-behaved kids. Yes, they are sweet and charming, but they were also so hard to control.

Josh thought I was too soft, but mostly, I'd just been in survival mode on my own and I couldn't get worked up about a lot of the things that bothered him. I didn't have the extra energy to waste on it.

I appreciated my parents sharing their fears, and I was heartbroken they were nervous and not as excited about the wedding as they'd led me to believe.

My mom had told me, "Dad is was having a hard time with this one (the wedding)," but I had no clue that translated to her too. She always seemed so impressed with Josh.

That night I spent a lot of time letting the Devil get the best of me, and I second guessed myself and my judgment. Was there something I didn't see? Was he not right for me? I started picking him apart and judging his every move with criticism. It felt awful and I spent the next few days asking for God to help me.

I completely understood my parents' fears about me getting married though. They had to take on so much to help me when Jeff left, and that in itself was hard. Watching my world fall apart was even harder, I'm sure. I can't imagine the pain I'd feel for Peyton or Ryan if they ever had to go through something similar.

What's different for me is that I spent more than a year healing with group therapy, support, and God, and I was able to learn and recognize so much to help me in the future. I felt completely sure of what I wanted and who I needed, and Josh matched it. He lived up to the high bar I required to bring a man into my life and the kids'.

All that time, my parents just had their usual routines. No time in church, no small groups, no education on divorce. I should never have assumed they were recovering like I was. How could they? Time heals wounds, but if you never treat that wound, the scar it leaves behind looks a lot worse.

Josh was not patient with the kids, and I fully recognized that. But I wasn't that patient either. There was just something different about me yelling at them vs a big six-foot-two man yelling at them. We both snap at them, and neither of us is perfect.

But Josh's life so drastically changed in the last twelve months, and considering that, I can't help but be SO PROUD of his engagement with them. I think it's unrealistic of me to expect he could love them like a dad when he had known them a year and wasn't with them since birth. But when I think about him knowing Ryan since before he was three and Peyton since she was five—that's *a lot* of years of them growing up for him to learn to love them like his own.

After I listened to my parents' concerns and thanked them for sharing with me, I went in and told Josh what had transpired. He was completely shocked this was about him. We talked about how he could engage with them better and I could tell he just had a million situations running through his head to play back, thinking of when he may have been in the wrong.

He admitted two powerful things to me that would be important for his growth as a parent and partner. First, he told me that when I would talk to him after he disciplined the kids in a way that I found too extreme, he usually didn't believe he'd been in the wrong. He believed it was an appropriate response or punishment. He said he'd try to take my opinion more seriously.

Second, he said that one of his problems was not treating each situation in isolation. If they'd been bad the day before or that morning, he brought that behavior into the current situation and reacted more strongly than perhaps he should. I thought this was a really powerful insight.

With kids, they move on so quickly and don't dwell on a lot or think about how they got in trouble for "X" yesterday and probably shouldn't do it again today. But Josh thought about it as a compounding situation, which made his reactions more intense.

After filling him in, Josh went out and talked to my parents. Because of course he would. He cared so much, and he didn't want them having any doubts about us or him. I didn't get any details from either party, but I prayed that it was sincere and effective and eased some of my parents' fears. Without God's presence in their lives though, and without some other form of support, I feared that it would just take time and silently watching and judging us for them to get secure.

———◆———

About a month later, I had one last piece of self-doubt creep in before our wedding.

A friend of mine from church, who had a similar story to mine, was happily remarried to another man and they'd had two more adorable kids together. They led a small group together and were just a gorgeous couple. The people you look at and think, "Wow, I want what they have."

I'd seen a post from her on Facebook that she was blindsided and needed prayer. When I saw her at church that day, I hugged her and asked if she needed to talk. "My husband told me he was cheating, and he's in love with her."

I was devastated. They seemed like a good couple who loved God and who was making it work, even when it was hard. I prayed for her during service and couldn't take my mind off her family.

Her first marriage was much like mine, and her ex even died too. I was so happy to see her have this second chance. Going into a second marriage, I think the thing we all think about is all the ways we're going to do it right this time. We would never get divorced again. Never make the same mistakes. Never allow the marriage to fall apart. And here she was. After doing all the right things.

I hated being at a place in life where this was reality. It was not fair. We go into marriage with such high hopes and dreams about our future, but then face the risk of it falling apart again.

I think what's odd is how hard it personally hit me. I still look at people like her who are in (what look like) successful second marriages, and I am expecting that happy ending for me and Josh. To see someone like them mess it up, and then to find out he'd cheated twice before. I couldn't stomach it. I could never picture Josh ever cheating on me, but does anyone? It's something like this that shakes you to your core, and it made me scared.

That couple ended up getting divorced and after an ugly battle, they're finally cordial. But the oldest daughter, from her first marriage, is the one I pray for most and think of often. I **ache** when I think of her. She'd been through this as a little kid, just like Peyton. I hate the idea of her as a teenager dealing with it all over again. She let this man into her life as her dad, and here he was, breaking her mom's heart—and hers too.

I continued to work through those fears and self-doubts through the fall, and in my heart of hearts, I knew everything I was doing was exactly what I was meant to do. It was all so full of God's love and I felt like I was just following this lit-up path all the way to my future.

I can't explain how I worked through my doubts. But so much of it was practicality. I really had spent the time to focus on what I wanted before Josh and I were even together. I knew exactly the type of man I wanted and needed. And that's what made it so easy to get serious with Josh after just a few months. He checked the boxes of what a good partner should be, and I knew I'd hit the jackpot. The kids had hit the jackpot.

Our wedding was a perfect day. I didn't have a concern or question about making this commitment, and that was the most comforting part. Stupidly, I still had fears and questioned if Josh would freak out and finally realize he couldn't do it, but that has subsided *mostly* since he officially said, "I Do."

Things were so happy and even peaceful. My life felt like everything was perfect, and that was a scary thought. My husband (HUSBAND!) loves me; he spends time with me, and I love having him in bed next to me even when he's snoring and keeping me from any decent sleep. I love that I don't have to question if he would take the kids to swim practice or help Peyton with her schoolwork.

Josh eases my fears and comforts me when I'm concerned, even when he thinks I'm crazy or he doesn't agree. He's solid and secure, but I hope he'll allow himself to be vulnerable with me too. I pray that he learns to let go and open up more, to let me take on some of his burdens so he doesn't have to carry the weight on his own. That's true partnership.

Chapter 25

Party of 5

We moved into our new home a few months after the wedding. It was truly a labor of love, and we thought about every detail.

About six months after the wedding, we went through another hard time with Peyton—one of many we're sure to face as she enters her teen years. She was in another phase of not wanting Josh around.

He had noticed, and after Father's Day that year he said, "Peyton and I don't seem to be connecting, and I don't like it. Ryan and I are in a good place, but she doesn't want anything to do with me."

My heart broke a little bit for this sweet and lovely family I'd been trying to concoct. He noticed that Peyton never wanted to call him Dad now. That she never wanted him to put her to bed. That she just generally gave him an attitude about things.

She'd started to tell me that Josh was her **stepdad**, not her dad. And telling me that she wished it was just me, her, and Ryan. Stepdad is a phrase we never used, so I know it's something she heard from school. And I'm sure all it took was one friend to say to her, "Oh he's not your dad. He's your stepdad." And that was it. She disconnected from their relationship.

What's worse, there's of course not a good explanation I can give a seven-year-old for why Josh is *so much better* for her life than Jeff ever could have been. There's no explaining to her that Jeff would have yelled at her so much more than Josh does. That he would never be there for her the way Josh wants to be.

So how do you walk that fine line of explaining to her without killing her idealized memories of her dad? You can't.

I told her I wanted to have a grown up talk with her. I asked her why she didn't want to be around Josh.

"I don't want to tell you," she said.

After some prodding, she finally admitted, "Because he's not my dad. And I want you to break up with him. I want it to be you, me, and Ryan again. It was easier that way."

So in my totally ineloquent way, I told her that life was NOT easy when it was just the three of us. I told her that our home wasn't very happy with Jeff in it either. That he wasn't always very nice to us. In her literal translation of that, she reminded me that Josh isn't always nice either (like punishing her or getting frustrated), so I tried and probably failed to explain it.

I told her that I'd asked Jeff to leave, and she was so upset and confused why I would want him to leave. And how do I explain this? It's complicated enough to adults, so HOW do you explain it to a kid?

I really struggled with mentioning the drinking at all because I didn't want her to look at me or anyone else who drinks and be scared something would happen to us. But telling her that Jeff didn't take care of himself and put things in his body that weren't healthy—well that didn't seem to cut it anymore.

It was time to tell her more.

Sometimes she felt so old to me, but other times, I knew she was still so innocent and sweet and didn't know anything about this world, even with what she'd been through.

This was a HARD age. She wanted to feel like a big kid but didn't have the emotional capacity to handle that. And explaining to her just how freaking lucky she was that her dad died would make absolutely no sense.

So I've instead sat in this awkward and sad holding pattern waiting for her to grow up and be able to comprehend it. There's nothing fun about focusing on that, but I also don't want to rush through this sweet part of her life. The sitting and waiting is unbearably hard. But sitting through your pain is a lot of what leads to the growth, to the understanding. Sitting with your pain and hurt ultimately leads to healing. And I suspect that will be the case for Peyton too.

Ryan is six now, and he still doesn't have any of the questions that Peyton has had. I think part of that is because Josh is all he knows. I haven't had to answer the tough questions yet with him.

———————◆———————

One night, I put Ryan to bed and then went in for Peyton's turn. But first I asked her to come in the extra bedroom and pray with me.

"Is this the prayer room?" she asked.

"No, you can pray wherever you want," I said. "But sometimes it's good to pray over exactly what you are hoping for. What do we hope this room becomes one day?"

"A BABY'S ROOM!" she said excitedly. "Will our prayers come true?"

"Well we don't get to decide that, and I've already been given you and Ryan, but I do know that God doesn't answer a prayer that isn't asked. I think we should just ask Him."

Then we sat across from each other on the floor, held hands, and closed our eyes.

Dear Lord,

Thank you for bringing together this family and bringing Josh into our lives to bless us in a way that we can't fully comprehend right now. We have so much love still to give and pray that you will soon fill this room with a crib, and baby clothes, and baby toys, and the sounds of baby cries and baby laughs.

Amen.

Then we went back to Peyton's room, and I asked if I could pray over her too.

Dear Lord,

Thank you for Peyton and her kind heart and big feelings. She is such a shining example of your grace and love, and I pray you will always be by her side through all of her struggles. She has a lot of feelings right now, and I pray that you help her sort those out and seek you first. Lord, encourage her to open up her heart to Josh. He loves her so much and wants so much to be a part of her life. Lord, I pray that you will bless Peyton and Ryan and may they always follow you and seek to have a heart like Jesus.

Amen.

She opened up to me a bit that night and told me that she hated Josh, which I told her we don't say about anyone, ever. And then she said she didn't love him and didn't care about him.

"But please don't tell him," she said. "I don't want his feelings to get hurt."

"Peyton, not wanting to hurt someone's feelings *means* that you care about them. If you hated him, you wouldn't care."

"He overreacts," she said.

That was true. He did get mad at them faster than I did, and because of his size, it felt all the more elevated. And it was hard to watch sometimes. Sometimes, it was deserved and they needed this kind of discipline. Other times, they were just being kids and he needed to cut them some slack. But every time, he was learning how to parent kids and get better at his job.

And more than anything for her, her love language is touch, and Josh isn't so good at that. He's not good at the hugs, the kisses, the back rubbing. These are easy things he can improve on though and hopefully he'd start to connect with her more often.

"I wish daddy was here. Why did you make him leave?" she asked desperately.

After some unsuccessful skirting attempts to tell her how her daddy was sick in his brain, I went for it.

"Do you want me to tell you how your daddy died?"

[head nod]

"Do you know what an addiction is?"

"No."

"Well, what's your favorite tv show?"

"Bunk'd," she said. (A Disney show)

"Okay, so you like to watch Bunk'd every day. And when you don't get to watch it for a few days, you really, really miss it, right? … Well that is how your daddy felt about alcohol. Now, alcohol, like beer, can be really bad for you if you have too much of it. It can start to change your brain and make you think you need to have it all the time. And that can be really bad for your organs inside your body. They can't handle too much of it, and if you have too much, you can get really sick. But when you're addicted, it's really hard to stop."

"So that's how he died? Why didn't you take him to the hospital?"

"I did try to help him. I sent him to a special place where they could take care of him, and even they couldn't make him better. Then I made him leave because I knew he loved me and you and Ryan more than anything in the world, so I figured that would stop him. And even that couldn't."

"So now that you love Josh, do you not love Daddy anymore?" she asked.

With her concrete thinking, loving Josh meant not loving Jeff and that felt wrong to her, so she felt like she needed to "hate Josh" to prove her love for her daddy.

She finally broke me, and I started crying. "That's not how it works," I told her. "I still love your daddy very much, but your daddy would want you and me to be happy and be taken care of. And me loving Josh doesn't mean I don't love Jeff. And you loving Josh doesn't mean you don't love Jeff."

"Well why do you call him Jeff and not Dad anymore?"

"Well, I do that because Josh is who is here now and he's who you will grow up with as your dad. Jeff will always be your daddy, but he wants you to be happy and have a dad to take care of you too. So it's okay."

She ended the night asking me to wake her when Josh came home so she could give us a hug.

By the time he'd returned home, I'd left her room but could hear her crying in bed. Josh went into her room and just laid with her and held her until she finally calmed down and fell asleep. From that night on, he said he's never felt like she had any of that animosity towards him. All it took was a little extra compassion and gentleness.

I know this won't be the end of it, since she learns a little bit more about alcoholism and Jeff each year, but I wonder if this was our turning point and the truth of knowing how Jeff died helped us. And even more important, knowing that loving Josh doesn't mean not loving Jeff.

———————— ◆ ————————

Shortly after, Peyton asked how people get a baby.

And cue the standard, "Well, when a mommy and daddy really love each other, they can make a baby…"

"And what about the kids?" she asked nervously. "Do the kids have to love the mom and dad too?"

"Well, of course. Everyone has to love each other to bring in a baby."

(Spoiler: At this point, I was eight weeks pregnant and about to work some mental magic on her that would play out when we actually told her.)

Then Peyton got a really scared look on her face and said she didn't love Josh. I told her that was okay, and her feelings would change. We'd had so much back and forth talking about her feelings and how she didn't always love him.

Then I stopped her. I told her that while she may feel that way today, she didn't feel that way a year ago when we got engaged, and I don't think she'll feel that way in the future. I reminded her how happy she was when we told her we were engaged and that the first thing she did was run to Josh and tell him, "I love you! Thank you! Can we keep you forever?"

And then in my head, I thought, "Wow, she'll know that she DOES love him when I tell her there actually is a baby in my belly."

We decided to tell Peyton on her birthday, with shirts for her and Ryan: "Big Sister Again" and "Big Brother Finally."

Peyton's reaction could not have been more beautiful. Usually, they always let me down when I film them expecting a great reaction for what they're about to get or see, but not this time. She showed genuine shock and excitement. And she even waited patiently to tell people until I told her it was okay. Ryan too!

Peyton was very attentive to what I ate and drank—making sure I didn't drink wine and I had plenty of water and milk. She was pretty hopeful for a girl early on, so I really focused on the positives of a brother so she wouldn't be let down—no sharing your clothes and still being my "favorite girl in the world" were the two main ones I went with.

Since I was "Advanced Maternal Age" for this pregnancy (I'd love to punch the man who came up with *that* medical term!), I got to do special blood work at 12 weeks, and one of the benefits is finding out the sex early. Is there a Y chromosome present, or not?

I somehow made it through an entire workday without logging in to view my test results and cheating to find out, and we all opened up an envelope together that afternoon. We let the kids open it, and before I could read the word, I could see the bright blue marker. A BOY!

I thought a boy was exactly what our family needed and couldn't have been more excited. He'd be closer in age to Ryan, and even though Josh claims I never would have known the difference, he really wanted a boy, so I was happy for him too.

Josh was amazing during pregnancy. I wish I'd taken advantage of his thoughtfulness more. It was the first time I didn't *completely* hate being pregnant and probably because I had a partner who was supportive and didn't make me feel bad about my changing body. I only sent him out to get me food twice—once for a jar of pickles and the other for some raspberries and blueberries. I was very conscious of my body this time around and stayed active at the gym and, aside from a new Skittles addiction, I ate pretty healthy. Funny enough though, I still gained fifty pounds. This further supports my theory that you're destined to gain a certain amount no matter what you do. I'd gained sixty with Peyton and fifty-five with Ryan too.

The best part of being pregnant was that Josh rubbed my feet on demand. By the last few months, it was literally every night. And he hates feet! I'm hoping I'll still get a least a few a year even though there are no more babies coming out of *this* body!

One of the best parts of this pregnancy was how meaningful it was. Of course, it was special for me and Josh and his family, but what really touched me was how much it meant to *others*, to anyone who'd been following my crazy life the last few years. I could see the sparkle in someone's eyes, the warmth from their heart, the feeling of hope rise in their bodies.

I refuse to use words like *happy ending* because my life isn't over and just when I get it figured out is when God upends it all, but to anyone looking through the door, a happy ending is exactly what they'd see. I continue to feel so blessed by all of those in my life, who have supported me and loved me through such difficult times, and this feels like my gift to them too.

———————— ◆ ————————

Our son Caleb joined our family last spring, and he completed us in the most perfect way. Peyton and Ryan love him dearly. They miss our bedtime routines that have had to change so I can feed the baby, but they've transitioned beautifully. Today is my final day of maternity leave, and I've used every free moment while he napped to work on this book.

My story has always been one I wanted to share, not only because it showed how God has better plans for you than you could have ever hoped to dream, but because I know that when you stop being embarrassed or ashamed of your circumstances, you can inspire others and help them too.

Josh and I are coming up on our two-year anniversary. Life has been far from perfect, but what I've learned this time around is to, in the words of Elsa, "Let it go."

It's hard to start each day with a clean slate. Really hard. I'm not perfect. Josh isn't perfect. And the kids certainly aren't either. But when something hurts, we try to talk it out—even if it's weeks after something has happened.

When I see someone going through a divorce, loss, or family turmoil of any kind, I am always quick to open my heart and let them in. To share parts of my story. It's only once we *share openly* that we can help others. And once we share, there's nothing left to be ashamed of.

I know there are countless stories out there like mine. Stories of women who have faced challenges they never thought would end, but they made it through. And like me, maybe they tried to find a community, find resources, a book, something... and nothing existed. I wanted it to exist. I wanted someone to read this book and find themselves nodding along thinking, "Me too! I thought I was the only one."

What you're facing financially or emotionally may be hard right now, but you will learn to adapt. You will find resources to help and you'll get creative. We're built for this.

What you're going through now may be *awful,* but it's not permanent. And when you make it through the other side of the door, when you feel yourself making progress, that's exactly when it's time to pay it forward.

Share your story. Keep it going. Your story is going to help someone else one day. Your story has strengthened you and built you into a more beautiful version of yourself.

And that right there makes all of this worthwhile. You're exactly where you're meant to be.

Acknowledgements

First and foremost, I must thank God for finding me and bringing me to him. I'd like to believe we would have found each other one way or another, but like so many, it took walking through the darkness to finally see the light. He is my comfort, my hope, and my joy.

Thank you to my parents. They have supported me at every stage of life. They set me free to wander the world as I wrapped up my college life, and when I wanted to marry Jeff at 22 years old, my parents welcomed him with open arms. They treated him like their own and provided him so much love and support.

When my world fell apart, they were a constant presence for me and the kids. Peyton and Ryan are loved every minute of the day by them and continue to be two of their favorite people ever.

Thank you to my friends—my Foxies, my work besties, and all of you who sent cards, texts, dinners, and just showed up to sit with me. I could not have survived without you.

To Josh, thank you for never playing games and for showing me and the kids what it means to love. You are an incredible man, and I cannot believe that God brought you to me. The kids and I are luckier than I could ever explain.

Thank you to my littlest man, Caleb. You haven't even said your first word yet, but you've already found your place in our home and hearts. I am so grateful I get to be your mom. I think you are going to be the glue of our family for years to come.

And finally, to Peyton and Ryan. The two of you are some of the kindest and bravest children I know. I hope one day you will see yourselves the way I see you. I love the love you have for each other. You are the best of friends, and I hope that never changes. My prayer for you is a lifetime of bravery, hope, and love. May you always remember your strength. You are not a statistic. You are children of God, and you have my endless love.

Suggested Resources

DivorceCare

To find a group in your city, visit DivorceCare.org

This is a Christian-based support group that I recommend to anyone going through a divorce. It **does not** matter if you go to church or not. You will absolutely find value in this video-based support group. Generally groups meet once a week (and most churches offer free child care!) and you watch that week's video and then spend some time talking about it or the things others are going through. It's really helpful to be able to ask questions about the legal system, custody, emotional concerns, and so much more! You can also sit quietly and not share at all! You'll still get so much value from it.

No groups near you? Sign up for their daily email list!

If your kids are elementary or older, they may also benefit from DC4K - DivorceCare4Kids. This is tougher to find, but if it's offered, it's usually at the same time as the adult session.

Banana Splits

https://www.bananasplitsresourcecenter.org

Banana Splits is a school-based children's group program for students who have experienced parental divorce or death. My kids weren't old enough to use this program, but it's been recommended to me by several people. Check with your child's school to see if they offer it.

Another option offered in elementary schools is a more generic "lunch group" with the school counselor. My daughter did this for two years, and they would focus on emotional health and growth—things like how to be a good friend and how to control your emotions.

ComfortZoneCamp
https://comfortzonecamp.org

ComfortZoneCamp is one of the most incredible organizations! It's a free weekend-long camp for children 7-18 who have lost a parent or sibling. Each child is partnered up with a 'big buddy' for the weekend, and they participate in small group therapy sessions with a trained grief counselor and mix in all the fun parts of a summer camp—ropes course, games, and bonfires!

Camps are currently offered in Virginia, New Jersey, and California.

Al Anon
https://al-anon.org

Think of it as Alcoholics Anonymous for the families. It's your safe place to go and sort through life with a partner or family member suffering from addiction.

YWCA

https://www.ywca.org

YWCA is available to help you with shelter, financial support, and counseling services.

Look for local non-profits in your area that specialize in things like domestic violence, child trauma, divorce, addiction, and any other area that may apply to you. I continue to be amazed at the number of local non-profits out there to help women and children. Even if your biggest concern is making sure your kids have a great Christmas—organizations are there to help people like YOU. Take advantage. Asking for help in your time of need is the best thing you can do for yourself and your children.

Recommended Books

For you:

Carry On, Warrior
by Glennon Doyle

I just adore this book. Glennon's writing style will have you laughing and crying on every other page. As a recovering alcoholic and bulimic, Glennon provides perspective that helped me understand more of what Jeff was going through. And her advice throughout the book provided me solace and strength during my most difficult season of life.

The Circle Maker: Praying Circles Around Your Biggest Dreams and Greatest Fears
Mark Batterson

If you're looking to grow in your journey with Christ, this is a great book to help you focus on prayer. It forces you to be disciplined and helps form the habit of prayer.

Modern Romance
Aziz Ansari, Eric Klinenberg

Because if you're going to be single again, this book will make you laugh.

The 5 Love Languages of Children
Gary Chapman, Ross Campbell

This book has the same love languages as its original version but focuses on children and their development. It really helped me identify my kids' needs and how to best show them love and discipline too.

Out of the Spin Cycle: Devotions to Lighten Your Mother Load
Jen Hatmaker

Jen is hilarious, and this is a book of short stories guaranteed to make you think and laugh.

How to Talk So Kids Will Listen and Listen So Kids Will Talk
Adele Faber, Elaine Mazlish

This is a great read to help you talk to your kids in general.

270

For the little ones:

There are many books out there for older children, but since mine were only one and four at the time of divorce, my recommendations focus on that age group.

When I Miss You (Way I Feel Books)
Cornelia Maude Spelman

The Invisible String
Patrice Karst

When Dinosaurs Die: A Guide to Understanding Death (Dino Life Guides for Families)
Laurie Krasny Brown

Inside Out Box of Mixed Emotions
Disney Book Group

As of publication, this box set of "emotions" is still in print. I read these books to my kids all the time. Each book focuses on one of the emotions from the movie. I found talking about feelings through the emotions used in the *Inside Out* movie to be incredibly valuable and effective for my little ones.

Works Cited:

Anonymous, Alcoholics. 1981. "Twelve Steps of Alcoholics Anonymous ." *aa.org*. Accessed 2019. https://www.aa.org/assets/en_US/smf-121_en.pdf.

Doyle, Glennon. 2014. *Carry On, Warrior.* Scribner.

Ellsworth, Tim. 2013. "Pat Summerall remembered for Christian faith." *bpnews.net.* April 17th. Accessed 2019. http://www.bpnews.net/40092/pat-summerall-remembered-for-christian-faith.

PaulaHenry1. 2011. "Absent Father: Advice For The Single Mom Without Dad." *Hubpages.com.* July 25th. Accessed 2019. https://hubpages.com/family/Absent-Father.

Sandberg, Sheryl. 3 June 2015. "Facebook Post Excerpt." Accessed 2015. https://www.facebook.com/sheryl/posts/10155617891025177:0.

Swift, Taylor. 9 June 2015. "1989 Concert Speech."

University, Stanford. 2019. "Alcohol & Drug Info." *alcohol.standford.edu.* https://alcohol.stanford.edu/alcohol-drug-info/buzz-buzz/what-bac.

Wevorce. 2017. "Why do Second Marriages Fail?" wevorce.com Accessed 2019. https://www.wevorce.com/blog/why-do-second-marriages-fail/

Zac Brown Band. "Chicken Fried." The Foundation, Atlantic Nashville, 2008.

Made in the USA
Middletown, DE
06 January 2020

Coles neuro-sx
apt @ UVA.

Denied: _____

Leah Burling
Managers Signature

1/20/2020
Date

Virginia Ear, Nose and Throat Associates, PC
Request for Paid Time Off

Name: Brandi Daniel ████████

Vacation Dates Requested: Leave @ 10:00 Date: 1-20-20 to: 1-23-20

Approved: ✓